THE
MANHUNTERS

THE MANHUNTERS

PETER DEELEY

The McCall Publishing Company
New York

Contents

Illustrations

between pages 96 and 97

KEY TO ACKNOWLEDGEMENTS
1   Ian Berry, Magnum
2   *Stern*
3   Associated Press
4   London Express News and Features
5   Associated Newspapers

Introduction

Detectives, by the very nature of their job, belong to a 'silent' service. Without secrecy a policeman would find it difficult to function effectively. This is why, despite the mass exposure of the detective in fiction—on film and in print—the man behind the police badge or the warrant card remains a remote, intangible figure.

The five stories in this book seek to bridge that gap. They are more concerned with the character and quality of the detective than with 'plot' or the personality of the criminals. Each policeman has stepped out of the shadows as it were to talk about himself and his job—the problems of crime-breaking, the fears of failure, the pressures for success.

Fiction has always cast the detective in the role of the hunter, the criminal as the quarry. The excitement of the chase has always fascinated man, probably more for the thrill of the hunt itself than the actual moment of entrapment. As Chitty, the Scotland Yard superintendent, remarks about the conclusion of a many months long hunt for a killer: 'It [the trial] was all an anti-climax.'

Emotion is a trap that the detective steels himself to avoid. Experience—mutilations, the physical or mental suffering of the victim—has drained the surface feeling from his nature. Only in this way is he able to dedicate himself to what is basically a distasteful job, pursuing fellow humans with the aim of depriving them of their liberty and even their lives.

He cannot allow himself to get involved emotionally in the crime he is investigating. Chitty had seen the murdered bodies of three fellow-policemen whom he knew personally.

Yet he had to bite back any personal hatred towards the killers: 'Once your judgement is clouded by emotion you are a liability to the men around you.'

In the French child kidnapping case, the agony of the parents was enough to ensure that Denis, the detective, never fell into the trap of sympathy for the offenders. Putting himself beyond emotion, the detective is in a better position to understand the criminal he is hunting. Eynck, of Germany, in investigating a series of baffling killings, admitted that at the end he had a kind of empathy for the murderer: 'The crimes he had committed were too horrible to forgive. Yet I understood enough of his upbringing to know why he turned out the way he did.'

Often, up to the moment of arrest, the suspect is at the most a name, a picture or a description; at the least, a fingerprint or a piece of hair. While he is shrouded in anonymity, the work of detection follows a set pattern — the eye-witness statements, house-to-house inquiries, forensic studies, the identification parade. But from the moment of confrontation onwards, when the criminal takes on an identity and it is his wit against that of the policeman, then the individuality of the detectives shows through.

In the Dutch smuggling and fraud case, it appeared at first to be the work of experienced 'white collar' criminals. When Toorenaar and Jagerman, the detectives, found the culprits, they discovered they were men who in essence were not far removed from themselves. The robbers were 'not criminals: playboys with a sharp sense of humour' and a strange friendship grew up between both sides.

What similarities there are between the policemen in this book — each at or near the top of his profession — lie in the universality of the 'tricks of the trade'. The differences are largely shaped by the rules of the legal system in which each operates.

Imundi, the New York homicide detective, explaining how he questioned a relatively unimportant witness, said: 'You must impress upon her that this is a routine thing. If you let your witness know your suspicions she may clam up on you and you will lose her confidence.'

It is a basic rule all these detectives obey that an interrogator must reveal as little as possible in his questioning of outsiders. Without colouring, without prompting, the detective will get the picture as the eye-witness saw it. That story may distort the facts as they are later established but at least it is the impression conveyed by the man on the spot. What that eye-witness says will from then on shape the first stages of the inquiry.

Dedication is another of the common factors which runs through each of the men's stories. In this work when the point of breakthrough is near it must be taken then or not at all. The Scotland Yard detectives spent days and nights without leaving the murder headquarters at the initial period of their investigation. By the time that pressure was off, the first of the killers was inside.

Denis, when he was questioning the kidnappers in the French Alps, had gone ninety-six hours without rest by the time he got the vital admission. If he had broken the continuity of his interrogation it would have given his adversary time to collect his wits and the psychological moment of breakdown might never have arrived.

But why such dedication? The monetary rewards alone do not justify it. In England, Holland, Germany and Canada salaries are roughly equivalent (about £3,000–£4,000 for the head of a detective division). In New York a senior detective may earn up to £7,000.* Denis, the Marseilles chief of police, was an exception. His salary, about £10,000, was supplemented by private consultancy work.

There is a sense of permanence and security in the police services that few other jobs can offer (a house, pension, a car for office time for senior ranks). But material rewards apart, there is little glory and even less popularity to inspire the would-be detective.

Unless they have family roots within the force, men gravitate towards policing largely by an accident of circumstances. Denis, a qualified lawyer, entered the job because it offered a way of escape from the Nazi forced labour camps; in very

* £ = $2.40

different circumstances, Chitty, the Londoner, came to the same conclusion — to escape his home environment he joined the Metropolitan force as a probationary constable.

But apart from security and this 'escape route', perhaps these men are drawn in part by the personal involvement the job offers. To the detective it is both essential and one of the more pleasant sides to his work to be always in touch with people. Where else would he be able to find his informants, get to hear what crimes are being planned, know where to look for the local criminals?

A detective must make himself all things to all people. As the American, Imundi, said: 'You've got to be able to sell yourself to the fellow at the corner frankfurter stand just as easily as you would to the university professor . . . You knock on a door and a man comes to it with his dog. It's a shaggy, smelling beast but it's his dog, probably the biggest thing in his world. So you must get into his avenue: "That's a beautiful dog you have".'

The successful detective has to be the most legitimate sort of 'con artist'. He must know a little about everything, understand how to spot the weaknesses in another person's make-up, have the personality to persuade some unknown first to talk, then to confide in him. The 'beautiful little dog' is the key which may unlock the door on a treasure trove of evidence.

But without informants, a detective is only half a policeman. The French kidnappers were positively linked to the crime for the first time by an informant who had seen them become wealthy overnight. In London, even before the first of the police killers had been arrested, informants were talking their heads off about the activities of three men known to be carrying guns.

Forensic evidence, for all its wide acceptance by the courts, still only plays a minor role in the construction of a case against a suspect. A court would be wary about convicting on the strength of only a bloodstain or a print without some circumstantial evidence to back it up.

Team-work is the essence of the successful inquiry and

detection today is more a matter of applying organisation and management. It is much less now the world where the 'sleuth's instinct' counts. Not that intuition based on years of experience is discounted: crime investigation, having no precise shape like the running of a business office, will always have a role for the man who works by touch rather than team decision.

But these detectives—with the exception of the American who had to 'play' all by instinct because of the nature of the crime—found themselves managing rather than detecting.

Chitty, with several hundred detectives under him to do the 'spadework', became almost a figurehead, acting as co-ordinator of everybody else's efforts. Toorenaar, in Amsterdam, turned himself and his office into a clearing house of information while men many thousands of miles away at the end of a telephone did the arresting and questioning.

Again Denis and Eynck, when they were given the task of trying to solve crimes others had failed, applied brain not brawn. Instead of rushing straight out to the crime scene they spent the first weeks of their assignment cut off from outside, reading and studying the case as it had been portrayed on paper.

This is probably the basic change in police methods today. Instead of the hunt being led from the front by the brilliant but unpredictable detective it is now led from the rear by the planner. Perhaps the image of the detective has lost some colour in this way but organised crime demands organised police work.

The feeling of 'friendly neutrality' that exists between the police and public in Britain is something that other countries still seek to copy. What are the reasons? Perhaps control of the police in a way that cuts the opportunities for corruption, the comparative absence of tensions between different communities, the belief in personal contact and the absence of guns.

Compare the willingness of the British public to show support for Chitty and sympathy for the men who died with Imundi, who met a wall of silence in his search for evidence in Mafia killings, or the population of Dusseldorf who—

probably with some reason—had lost faith in the ability of the police to stop the slayings.

Chitty alone, of all these detectives, had never used firearms. Imundi, in New York, on balance felt that it would be a step forward to ban guns 'on both sides'. But, he asked: 'How and when do you call the truce?' None of the policemen could imagine a climate of police-public relations in which law and order could be kept without the threat of guns. 'When a killer pulls a gun on you there is only one way to stop him' was the gist of their argument.

Differences in method of detection are largely influenced by the legal systems in which detectives operate. A 'holding charge'—a petty offence which is later dropped—is a device by which the British policeman can get a suspect held in custody. But he would never be able to go as far as Eynck, the German, who when he found his suspect already in prison was to continue the detention beyond the period of the original sentence by virtue of a warrant holding him as a material suspect.

Compare that with the situation which faced Denis in France. Having begun his interrogation with the kidnappers he had forty-eight hours in which to obtain an admission. After that he was bound to go to an examining magistrate who would take over the inquiry or let the suspects go.

In Amsterdam, Toorenaar admitted that he had more latitude than his colleagues abroad. First he was able to enter a suspect's room without authority, then detain the man for four days without needing to call in a defence lawyer.

Chitty, in London, was well aware of the risks he was running by detaining his suspect for nearly three days without direct evidence linking him with the police killings. A suspect, under British law, must be brought before a court at the earliest possible moment after he is charged. Chitty had got to the moment where he either had to charge the man or let him go. Instinct guided him to charge. That instinct worked: the suspect broke and admitted his guilt.

Theorists may reasonably object to a man's liberty depending

on another's intuition. Yet much police work must continue
to be rule-of-thumb because the issue is rarely clear-cut—one
man's word against another with forensic evidence tilting the
balance.

Eynck and Denis were both called in to investigate complex
crimes after the failure of other detectives. In Germany this
system of 'warming up' old unsolved cases is often used. The
idea was anathema to Chitty at Scotland Yard whose view,
held by all policemen, is that it is crucial to enter the case at
the earliest possible moment. Again first impressions are as
important as they are with the eye-witness.

In varying degrees, the climax of the investigations was the
first confrontation between hunter and hunted. Chitty, when
he saw the third of the police murderers, felt a loathing; Denis
sensed the drama of the moment almost overcoming him as
he sat across the table from the leader of the kidnapping gang.
But to carry out their interrogations, both men had to wipe
their minds clear of personal emotion.

The ability to make another human confess his life away—
the collision of two wills—without recourse to force, is the
culmination of the art of the good detective. It is a question
of knowing what questions will break that mind, what atmo-
sphere to create—one of tension and hostility or compassion.
And it is the skill of summing up your man before you even
open your mouth.

Eynck knew interrogation was a waste of time when he
sensed the acute hostility of the suspect.

But for Denis, the interrogation was the centre-piece of the
whole affair. His examination was a *tour de force*, an immense
exercise in mental persuasion which left him as drained of
spirit as the criminal. Imundi had to rely solely on a series of
informal 'chats' with his suspect to dig through to the answer.

In the Scotland Yard case there was abundant proof—yet
Chitty wanted a confession out of the mouths of the men
themselves to make absolutely certain of conviction.

The Amsterdam detectives, on the other hand, had only
one sure way of clearing up the involved story of gold

smuggling—by persuading the men they held in custody to tell the full story. By finesse, bluff—even 'tea and sympathy' —they broke down a man who had sworn not to say a word.

These then are the skills of the 'Manhunters'—students of human behaviour at its lowest ebb. They deserve credit for at least 'touching pitch' and remaining human.

MATHIAS EYNCK: GERMANY

The Dusseldorf 'Doubles' Killer

The Dusseldorf 'Doubles' Killer

In Germany they call Mathias Eynck 'the specialist in unsolved crimes'. This slightly-built, studious man has an enviable reputation as a crime-breaker. Murder is his *forte:* only one of the fifty killings he has investigated remains unsolved.

Eynck, now C.I.D. chief for the North Rhein Westfalen department, knows the identity of the one man who has escaped his grasp. 'It was a homosexual killing. Somebody whispered a name to us but we were never able to make it stick."

His office at police headquarters is spotless, airy and quiet. His desk is as tidy, the papers as precisely ordered as the man himself. Nowadays he involves himself very little in day-to-day crime inquiries. As chief of the C.I.D. in this bustling, fast-growing industrial area, he administrates and co-ordinates. For one who spent many of his thirty-four years in the police 'out on the road' this role is rather irksome at times.

But today, at fifty-five, he is at the age when he can look forward to a peaceful retirement away from the sordidness of a job that seems alien to a man of his gentle charm.

He will also be able to look back to the high point of his career: when he matched his skills as an investigator against those of a mass killer who boasted — and almost proved — that he was beyond the reach of the law.

Few detectives, given the peculiarities of the crimes and the overpowering personality of the criminal, could have succeeded. Eynck did. But first he had to rectify errors which other policemen had made, mistakes which badly hindered the work of catching the killer.

The case of the Dusseldorf 'doubles' murderer Werner Boost proved one thing: that even with the apparatus of modern crime detection, trapping the criminal depends upon the ability of the detective who is pursuing him. And policemen, though they may carry a gun or a warrant card, are only fallible.

When Eynck, at that time a chief inspector, was called from Dortmund to neighbouring Dusseldorf in 1956 to try to halt a spate of killings which had shocked all Germany for four years, he was being given an unenviable task: to resurrect crimes whose trails had run cold long ago and in so doing provide answers to questions which had already defeated three other detectives.

Dusseldorf police had lost the confidence of the public because of the killer's apparent immunity to capture. Over a period of years three men and two women had been murdered, three others attacked. All were couples: this was the one linking feature, all overpowered as they sat at night in lonely spots by the side of the Rhine or in the woods surrounding Dusseldorf.

Besides this there was another very special reason for the unease of the Dusseldorfers. Once before this city—ancient state capital and modern powerhouse of industrial Germany— had experienced the dread of a phantom mass murderer.

There were many areas of similarity between the Kurten case and that of Werner Boost, in the manner of the crimes, the personality of the killers and the police investigations.

❧Peter Kurten, the 'Monster of Dusseldorf', probably ranks with Jack the Ripper and Henri Landru, the French 'blue-beard', as the outstanding mass murderers of modern times. Kurten was twelve when his family moved to Dusseldorf but according to his own confession, his first killings had taken place at the age of nine when he pushed two boys into the Rhine.

In 1913 he committed his first sexual murder, killing a young girl in her sleep after he had broken into her parents' home to rob. In the same year Kurten attacked four other women and a man, none of whom died. After the war Kurten returned to Dusseldorf and began a reign of terror. In the next three years, by his own account, he attempted to strangle four women and started seventeen fires.

In 1929, innocent blood ran as red as the sunsets which Kurten used to delight in seeing. There were eight murders and fourteen attacks in ten months. Two children were attacked together, strangled and their throats cut. An anonymous letter written to a local paper pin-pointing the burial spot led to the uncovering of another body on meadowland close to the Rhine.

An attack which failed on a servant-girl led to Kurten's arrest—an arrest as bizarre as the life he led. The girl took police to where he lived. Kurten saw them coming, sought out his wife and confessed to her that he was the 'monster' so that she could claim the reward for his capture.

While in custody awaiting trial, Kurten readily agreed to be examined by a psychiatrist to help explain the motives which impelled him to murder.

Kurten said that the sight of blood or a fire always produced in him an orgasm. It became clear that a depraved sexual lust mixed with a desire to revenge himself upon society for its treatment to him as a child were the primary motives.

After a ten day trial, Kurten, who had pleaded insanity, was found guilty of nine murders and sentenced to death. He was executed in July, 1931 — when Werner Boost, illegitimate son of a peasant girl, was only three years old.

Kurten, like Boost after him, was a respectable family man outwardly. But his criminal acts were legion. Apart from murder and assault, he robbed, burned and committed acts of beastiality with animals.

Boost, besides being a multiple killer, lived in a dream world where he created complex schemes to attack people and steal from them or kill. He too turned to arson in one case, to hide the identity of a couple he murdered.

The appalling conditions of Kurten's childhood, drunkenness, fighting, incest, a family history of mental retardation, undoubtedly helped to create the monster that he became. Eynck believes that Boost's childhood too, as disordered and insecure as that of Kurten — though without the overtones of brutality—undoubtedly contributed to his devious personality. 'I could never find it in me to pity Boost. He inflicted the most awful suffering on innocent people. But at least by the end of the case I felt I understood what drove him to it—his disturbed upbringing.'

In the Kurten case the motives were primarily sexual—the killings showed clear evidence of sadism and in at least one case necrophilia. Eynck's view of Boost is that the crimes he committed were again an expression of sexual depravity. Many of the facts suggest that Boost got an intense pleasure out of the suffering he inflicted on others.

Even in the police investigation of the two criminals—each man set in a decade when Germany was recovering from the aftermath of defeat in war—the stories overlap in many details.

Because of an error by a junior clerk in the Dusseldorf police records bureau, a tip from a member of the public that Kurten was the monster was disregarded. It was ignored because a report by a girl that Kurten had attacked her occurred at a time when the records showed he was in jail. In fact the entry in the records was incorrect: Kurten was 'on the loose' at the time. (Three people denounced Kurten to the police. One woman who had been assaulted by him and thrown into the river was fined for 'gross nonsense'. Only on appeal did she get the conviction quashed.)

It was an error by a Dusseldorf police officer which allowed Boost to go undetected when evidence of his guilt literally lay in the hands of the authorities. The gun he used in his first murder was found very close to his home and handed in to the police. It was not tested because of its dilapidated state until four years later.

This mistake allowed Boost to remain free to carry out four more killings: the error in the records office in 1929 gave Kurten time to commit at least another five sadist murders.

After the failure of the original investigators to catch Kurten, Inspector Gennat was brought in from Berlin to lead the inquiry.

Gennat was famed for his thoroughness. In one case he had

followed up 800 clues to catch a murderer. Inside a year of his arrival in Dusseldorf, Kurten was in prison.

Eynck, murder-hunter extraordinary, was summoned to Dusseldorf to head the murder team after the local authorities, disturbed by the failures to catch the killer, had ordered a reshuffle of the murder squad. Eynck too relies on thoroughness: 'I must get deep down into a case, take it apart on paper and put it together again before I am prepared to go out and begin the active part of my investigation.' Six weeks from the date of his attachment in Dusseldorf Eynck had obtained a 'holding warrant' for Boost's detention as a prime suspect in the five murders.

.   .   .

Eynck doubts whether Boost was consciously trying to emulate Kurten. 'I think personally that it is unlikely because he was neither of Kurten's generation nor of his time in the general sense.

'But it was a different matter in the minds of the public. As each murder outstretched the last in horror, people became very agitated. The older generation who could remember the Peter Kurten case had the idea that his ghost had risen from the grave: that it was a reincarnation of the monster.'

But Eynck knew he was dealing with no spirit from the dead, even though the murders he was trying to solve stretched back into the dim past. In one sense, Eynck only entered the story at the last act. But without his presence it is unlikely there would have been any denouement.

The following pages detail the dossier of fact and speculation which Eynck took to his home to read—and from which he built the evidence to nail Boost—when he first entered the inquiry in November, 1956.

The first date in the file was January 17th, 1953. A heavy storm of snow had swept across western Europe and by night the countryside around Dusseldorf was a white, frozen land. The streets, even the bars of the city, were deserted as all but a few souls had taken to their homes.

But in the Rotterdamer Strasse, a quiet, tree-lined road running north out of Dusseldorf along the right bank of the Rhine, an Opel Kapitan was parked on the verge beneath a clump of trees. Sitting in the front were two men, Dr. Bernd Servé, a lawyer, and beside him, in the passenger's seat, nineteen-year-old Adolf Hüllecremer.

Four hundred metres away, two more men were strolling across fields which led past a derelict brick kiln and on towards the street. They were work-mates at a metal factory and both were keen animal hunters. One was Werner Boost, the other a man we will just call Franz. Today, he has served his sentence for his part in the crimes that follow and has now settled down in a new life in another part of Germany.

It was just before eleven o'clock on that cold, inhospitable night. As yet neither of the two groups of men was aware of the other's existence.

With Eynck's help we can now fill in the gaps which he found when he first came to study the case. Early the next morning when Dusseldorf police arrived at the scene they found Dr. Servé dead and Hüllecremer distraught, shaking with fright and physically hurt.

The lawyer was lying across the front seats of the car, a bullet through his head. His coat and briefcase were on the back seat.

There was a good deal of blood splashed around the front of the vehicle from the mortal wound in Dr. Servé's head. Snow, drifting in from the open doors, had settled and was beginning to melt.

Hüllecremer told the police that he and Dr. Servé had been talking when the driver's door was suddenly pulled open. A man stood there with a gun in his hand and a mask over the lower portion of his face, covering nose and mouth.

Almost instantaneously it seemed to Hüllecremer, his own door was wrenched open and a shot went off into Dr. Servé from close range. There had been no warning, not a word had been spoken.

Hüllecremer, terrified by what had taken place, looked to his right and saw another masked man also carrying a gun.

Hüllecremer instinctively put up his hands, to ward o
expected bullet and partly as an act of surrender. All he
remember shouting was: 'No, no.'

But instead of the bullet, his assailant bent down and w...-
pered in his ear: 'Put your head down. I won't do anything to
you.'

Hüllecremer covered his head with his hands. He was too
petrified to move or to observe what the man who had shot
Bernd Servé was doing.

Again his attacker whispered in a very low voice: 'Bend
down, you idiot. Nothing will happen to you.' Then as
Hüllecremer tensed himself to receive the bullet, he felt instead
a crack—from the butt of the gun—on his head and lurched
forward in the seat.

Boost, the man who had shot Servé, gesticulated across the
prone bodies of the two men at Franz. He pointed a finger at
the inert Hüllecremer and ordered: 'Go on, put him under.'

At this moment Hüllecremer tried to sit up. He groaned:
'Let me live, let me live, I won't give you away.' He felt three
or four more cracks on the top of his skull and collapsed forward again, momentarily losing consciousness.

After a few seconds he came to and found himself still living
the nightmare. The voice in his ear whispered: 'Pretend you
are dead.' For the first time, the instinct for survival overcame
the terror which had clogged Hüllecremer's mind. He sensed
that he was being given the chance to live and became still.

Half-seated, half-kneeling in the car seat, Hüllecremer felt
a heavy weight across his back. Though he could not then make
out what it was, it was the body of his friend Dr. Servé. Then
the impediment was lifted from him—Boost had pulled the
body upright again to search its pockets.

Then Boost turned to Hüllecremer and began to go through
his pockets. Hüllecremer felt that he was now on the edge of
death. Something told him this was the man who had already
killed once: there was nothing to stop him killing again to
wipe out the only eye-witness.

The hand ceased its probing, withdrew the wallet, and

then once more the dead weight of the lawyer fell across Hüllecremer. He sensed that somebody had got into the driver's seat and was trying to start the car. But after a few moments that too stopped. He heard a voice shout, 'Let's go,' and then there was complete silence.

When Hüllecremer eventually pulled himself out of the car he saw Servé's body lying across the driver's seat. But the attackers had gone.

Four years later, Hüllecremer faced his assailants at an identification parade at Dusseldorf police station. But time, and the fear which had gripped and paralysed his mind that night, made it impossible for him to pick out either man.

.   .   .

To the Dusseldorf police the motive for the crime was clearly robbery. The killers had taken Dr. Servé's wallet together with Hüllecremer's and had got away with several hundred Deutschmarks. But they had probably got scared before they could search the bodies and the car more thoroughly: the lawyer's briefcase had not been tampered with.

But there was no such straightforward explanation for the killers' attempt to start the car. Presumably they had failed because they had been unable to find the starter—on this particular model it was mounted on the floor. They might have wanted to move the car and its occupants to delay discovery of the crime.

The pathologist's examination of Dr. Servé's body confirmed that the lawyer had died instantly from a gunshot wound. The shot had entered at the left side of the jaw, had travelled upwards at a forty-five degree angle and had exited through the right temple.

The bullet which the police recovered at the scene was to be their one tangible clue. It had been fired from a relatively unusual type of pistol, an 08 (the year in which it was first made), a nine millimetre calibre, widely used by the German forces in the First World War.

An appeal was put out to the public asking for all guns which had been found since the murder to be handed in. Four weeks later, in February, 1953, Helmut Pascher, a scrap dealer, was poking among rubble in a field on the outskirts of Dusseldorf when he unearthed the remains of a pistol. It was in pieces, dirty and unworkable and turning rusty. When reassembled, the firing pin of the pistol, an 08, was missing. Pascher recalled the police appeal and handed it in.

He had found the gun in the Theveser Feld—a large plot of land where refugees from the east and families whose homes had been destroyed in the last war had built themselves temporary accommodation. Among the families living in Theveser Feld was Werner Boost, a twenty-five-year-old metal worker, his wife Hanna and their two little daughters.

In a lost-and-found book Dusseldorf police recorded the handing in of the gun and the date: February, 1953—Theveser Feld. The pistol was passed on to the technical department. It was examined more closely but appeared to be quite unserviceable. From its condition it looked as though it had been buried for a long time before being dug up by Pascher.

A gun involved in a shooting crime may reveal two types of clue. In a clean state externally it may carry the prints of the hand that held it. In any event, every gun has its own identifiable characteristics—the marks from inside the barrel which are called 'lands and grooves'.

The 08 pistol found in Theveser Feld obviously could tell nothing of the man who had used it. But there was still the chance of establishing the markings inside the barrel. Where a gun is in an unworkable state it can still be operated by adding parts from other weapons, here the firing pin. Then the gun is fired into sand, the bullet extracted and under the microscope it will be seen to bear the tell-tale lands and grooves from inside the barrel.

In the Dr. Servé case none of this routine procedure was carried out with the Theveser Feld pistol. Instead a label was tied to the gun: 'Unable to test: firing pin is missing'. Then it was placed in a box alongside other weaponry handed in by

the public and placed in a store cupboard in the police headquarters. Karl Leitz, the detective in charge of the Servé
murder, was never told of its discovery.

It remained there for four years—only brought to light from
its dusty hiding place by Eynck when he was picking his way
through a series of apparently unrelated crimes.

Between January, 1953 and November, 1955 the Servé
murder faded from memory. Even for the police the job of
finding the killer was gradually dropped down the list of
priorities as more immediate work came to the fore.

The link between Dr. Servé and the crimes which happened
thirty-four months later might never have been established but
for one common factor, the Rotterdamer Strasse. This street is
Dusseldorf's equivalent of the ubiquitous 'lovers' lane'. Its
peace, its shelter and its situation away from the centre of
population make it a popular spot for couples.

On November 1st, 1955, Dusseldorf police were told that a
couple, Friedhelm Behre, aged twenty-six, a baker and his
twenty-three-year-old girlfriend Thea Kürmann had failed to
return home the previous night. They had last been seen alive
at 12.30 a.m. that morning in a bar in Dusseldorf. They had
left together in Behre's light blue Ford car.

For a month there was no trace of the couple.

Superintendent Josef Botte, the head of the Dusseldorf murder
squad, first explored the possibility that Behre might have
killed the girl, disposed of her body, and then made off in his
car. All police and frontier posts were circulated with a description of the couple and the two-door saloon. A love letter
from Behre to the girl was found and handed to Botte. In it
Behre talked about the idea of them running away together.
This was another possibility—a voluntary elopement—that
Botte had to reckon with.

Questioning Behre's former girlfriends, Botte found that he
always did his courting in a car parked in the Rotterdamer
Strasse. It seemed probable that he and Thea Kürmann had
gone there from the bar the night they disappeared.

They had left the bar at about twelve-thirty a.m. and would

have arrived in the Rotterdamer Strasse by twelve-forty-five. But from that time on the couple and their car seemed to have vanished from the face of the earth.

Then on November 28th, 1955, as the wet weather which had plagued the area in the past few days relented and the waters began to recede, a lorry driver passing through the outskirts of Kalkum, a small town about nine miles north of Dusseldorf, spotted the glint of metal through some trees.

It came from a gravel tip which had been filled with rain water. But the water had drained away and now the roof of a blue car could be seen breaking the surface.

A towing wagon pulled the car out of the water. When the driver looked inside he could make out the shape of two bodies lying on the floor under the back seat. Behre and Kürmann had been found.

The pathologist, Professor Böhmer, was at the Opera in Dusseldorf when a message arrived from the police half-way through the performance asking his attendance urgently at the mortuary. His post-mortem examination of the bodies showed that both had been attacked and that a succession of blows had been rained on them with a blunt instrument. Their skulls had been badly fractured.

But one astonishing fact emerged. The head injuries had been inflicted at least half an hour before death. The couple had died from drowning. They had still been alive, though probably unconscious, when driven into the water-filled tip.

Botte was certain that they had been surprised while sitting in the van in the Rotterdamer Strasse. They had been beaten over the head with a heavy iron tool of some description. But how had they first been subdued? Were there two attackers? Or had a gun been used to frighten them into compliance?

After the attack the killer or killers had gone through their clothing. Behre's mother told the police her son usually had about £10 on him and the girl about £4. No money was recovered from the bodies but the girl's jewellery, including her ring, had been left behind.

The night the crime must have taken place was very dark and misty. That had helped the killer to cover his tracks. But at the same time it must have required intimate local knowledge of the geography of Kalkum to locate the gravel pit. It was situated well back from the road and anybody not familiar with the area would never have seen it in the fog. The killer must have manhandled the car into the water and then returned—to Dusseldorf?—on foot.

The police were forced to ask themselves what manner of man could have undertaken such a journey, crouched over the headlights of a strange car with the unconscious bodies of his victims behind him looking for a spot in which to hide them and the vehicle. Almost certainly it was not just a thief, not even a thief who had panicked. The degree of callousness suggested a link with the Dr. Servé crime; that and the spot at which the attack had probably taken place. And each was a car murder. But the motives were too disparate at this stage to establish a positive connection.

While the detectives were still pondering over these questions, the work of their ten-week-old investigation was overtaken by the report of a second double killing. Again a car was involved. And again it started off as a missing persons report.

.   .   .

On the night of February 7th, 1956, Peter Falkenberg, aged twenty-six, a professional driver, and his girlfriend of a few weeks Hildegard Wassing, a twenty-year-old typist, had gone to a dance together in Falkenberg's black Mercedes 170S. When they failed to return home. Wassing's mother rang the police.

The police established that the couple had last been seen in Dusseldorf at ten o'clock the previous night. This time they did not have to wait long for developments. During the day the car was found abandoned in Dusseldorf's Altstadt (old city). Blood, in large quantities, covered the back seats.

Botte, at murder squad headquarters, took over the inquiry

on February 8th. The ingredients for murder were obvious. But where were the bodies?

Twenty-four hours later, a report from the village of Ilverich, close to Dusseldorf, provided the answer to this latest mystery. A gardener cycling to work had spotted a burnt-out hayrick behind the village. When he got off his bicycle to investigate, he had seen a blackened hand protruding from under the charred straw. The police lifted the remains of the rick and found Falkenberg and Wassing underneath.

Both bodies were burnt almost beyond recognition. Wassing's wrist-watch was identified by a member of her family: her dentist recognised work he had carried out on her teeth. Falkenberg was identified by a bunch of keys and a shoe repair ticket which had somehow escaped the blaze.

The police pathologists were able to say that this time both had died from a series of blows to the head with a heavy instrument. But in Falkenberg's case, the man had been shot before death from close range with a small calibre — 5·6 mm. — pistol. The bullet was found still lodged in his head.

The doctor who examined Falkenberg's body had carried out the post-mortem on Dr. Servé over three years before. He recalled the path the bullet had taken in the lawyer's case. He told the police that the shot fired at Falkenberg had been delivered at exactly the same angle — forty-five degrees, travelling upwards from the left chin to the right temple.

Hildegard Wassing had been raped before she was killed. Her hands were tied together with a piece of clothes line — fortunately for the police enough of the rope had escaped the blaze for them to preserve it as evidence — and her own scarf had been tied around her mouth.

One curious feature was the use of a rubber ring, the type normally found on jam jar lids for use as an air-tight seal. This had been placed vertically round the girl's head, running from the forehead round the chin. It looked as though it had been placed there to keep the scarf-gag from slipping.

The police surmised that the attack had not taken place at the spot where Falkenberg and Wassing were found. They had probably been parked nearby, somewhere on the left bank of the Rhine closer to Dusseldorf. The murderer had first shot Falkenberg, gravely wounding but not killing him. Then he had tied up the girl and attacked her. After that, with both victims at his mercy, he had killed them with repeated blows to the head.

The next move had been to drive them in the Mercedes— the amount of blood on the back seat suggested they had lain there some time—to Ilverich. Carrying both bodies across the field, he had buried them under the hay. Then, as if to make a final demonstration of his cold-bloodedness, he had taken the Mercedes and used it to drive himself back to Dusseldorf.

The gardener told Botte that he had noticed the burnt-out haystack the previous morning but had not then bothered to stop and investigate.

Everything pointed to the fact that they had already been dead beneath the rick that morning, even before the blood-stained car was found in the Altstadt. Tests established that petrol, possibly taken from the fuel tank of Falkenberg's car, had been used to set the rick alight.

The four murders appalled the police and public alike. Each time it seemed that the killer had been able to get several hours' start before the discovery of the crime. Was it just luck, or was it planning—or was it indeed Peter Kurten come back to life?

Dr. Wehner, the head of the Dusseldorf C.I.D., launched the Rheinland's biggest-ever manhunt. A reward of £1,500 was offered for information leading to the detention of the killer; the murder teams were split up and strengthened, each squad concentrating on one aspect of the inquiry and four million questionnaires were distributed to the public.

The pace of the job was telling on the policemen who had been involved non-stop for four months. Superintendent Botte's health gave way. He went on convalescence for two months and his position as overall head of the murder squads was given to Superintendent Stradmann.

.   .   .

prison in June, 1956 for six months. Officially he had been cleared of any connection with the killings. Dusseldorf police explained publicly that he was not the man they were searching for, just a poacher. But for Stradmann and his colleagues he remained a vital suspect.

The offence of trespass in the wood was in effect a holding charge.

Dr. Wehner, the head of Dusseldorf C.I.D., a criminologist with an international reputation, knew that he had until December to pin the killings on Boost. After that time the man would be free to destroy all evidence that remained to connect him with the crimes—even to the extent of liquidating any accomplices.

Wehner instructed his officers to continue their inquiries on the supposition that Boost might be the murderer. But this effort produced nothing which could stand the test of scrutiny by defence lawyer.

At the beginning of November, 1956, with time rapidly running out for the Dusseldorf police, the district department responsible for police affairs ordered a reshuffle of the murder team. Dr. Wehner approached an old colleague and asked him to take charge. From Dortmund, Mathias Eynck, then a chief inspector, drove over to Dusseldorf to make his first acquaintance with the man dubbed the modern day Peter Kurten.

.   .   .

Only a slight limp today betrays the two war wounds Mathias Eynck carries round with him from his service as a German infantry officer in the last war. Eynck, called up for military training four weeks before the outbreak of hostilities. served in Norway and Russia as well as the home front.

Shot twice, in the hip and in the thigh, he finds the effort of standing for long periods fatiguing. But physical stamina alone has never played an important part in Eynck's approach to his job. In this, the most difficult assignment of his career, he began by shutting himself off from the outside world for four weeks.

To the quiet of his Dortmund home Eynck brought all the papers and police reports of unsolved crimes in the Dusseldorf area dating back to 1950. Each day he worked from breakfast time until one o'clock the next morning, studying and memorising. 'When I got to bed I couldn't sleep for thinking about the case. If you had woken me up in the middle of the night and asked for a specific fact I could have quoted it to you chapter and verse.'

Eynck did not delude himself about the magnitude of the task. He was being asked to recreate events which had happened as far back as four years ago.

'Every detective ideally likes to begin at the beginning. If you see the body, the spot where it lay, the surroundings, they can tell you something.'

But here there had been a complete breakdown and the murder specialist had to reconstruct each case in his mind.

The reconstitution of a murder team is a normal feature of German police work. Eynck calls it: 'Warming up a case. We do this as a matter of routine. In the Boost case, as it happened, the investigations were still warm. But even where the crimes are ten to twenty years old you will find new squads being called in.'

Eynck believes that apart from the difficulties for a detective in coming 'second-hand' to a crime, the system has its advantages. 'A detective finds, I have found it myself, that if you spend too long with a case you become a little bit blind. Your mind "walks" in one direction; your brain no longer has the freshness to absorb new ideas. You become stale. And this is the worst thing that can happen to an investigator. If you change the investigator there is always the chance that he will see something you have overlooked.'

At the end of a month of concentrated homework, reading himself into the inquiry, Eynck was left with two principle features: Boost, a man with many question marks against his name but a man who would not talk; the feeling that many of these crimes were the work of two men.

Besides this, there were a number of circumstantial links between Boost and the various attacks:

His excuse that he was hunting animals when arrested by ranger Spath at Meererbusch. 'This was a strange set-up. Why push a motor-bike in there? It was very wet in the wood, not the place for a motor-bike and not the weather for shooting game. I came to the conclusion that only the presence of mind of the forester had prevented another double murder that evening.'

Inquiries had revealed that Boost was an expert marksman—that he could hit a target several yards away without taking the gun from the holster at his waist. 'The angle of the bullet in the Dr. Servé and Falkenberg murders suggested that the gun had been fired when the killer was crouching or that it had been fired upwards from waist level.'

It had been a very foggy night when the killer drove Behre and Kürmann from the Rotterdamer Strasse to the gravel pit at Kalkum. 'We figured it must have needed someone with local knowledge to find the tip. I learned that Boost had been brought up in a children's home in that area and had often been in the vicinity of the gravel tip when he was hunting for game.'

Eynck decided to confront Boost in jail. 'As soon as I went into the room he pulled a newspaper cutting out of his pocket.'

It was the story about Boost being questioned by the police as the murder suspect when he was first arrested. 'He held the paper up to my face—the headline said something about him having been cleared of suspicion—and shouted: "What do you want? The other police have already cleared me. They don't think I'm the wanted murderer."

'I tried to talk to him but he would not "come over". In the end he refused to be interviewed by me. He said it was because I was trying to incriminate him but I think he knew that we were starting to collect a mass of evidence and that he would not be able to put up any defence if we confronted him with it.'

Now Eynck concentrated on finding Boost's partner-in-crime. He went to see Mrs. Boost and asked her who had been her husband's friends. She mentioned a few names, among them Franz. He was placed under close observation but the days went by without anything happening to arouse the suspicions of the watchers. Finally, Eynck questioned Franz. 'We knew he had once been in trouble for poaching, but otherwise he was of good character. He came from a solidly religious family.'

Franz told the detective that he had worked at the same factory as Boost, had known him since 1952 but said the friendship had broken up.

Eynck was on the verge of giving up this particular trail when he came across a tiny, but terribly significant point. It was to turn the whole course of the case. He found that Franz was paying Mrs. Boost money while her husband was in jail. Why should a casual acquaintance, somebody who was not well off himself, be doing this?

On the strength of this link, Franz's house was searched. A pair of opera glasses and a few cheap pieces of jewellery were found. They matched the police list of articles stolen from a shop in Buderich in January, 1956.

Without needing to look at his files, Eynck remembered the details of the break-in. Guns had been stolen too, including a 5.6 mm. pistol of the type which had shot Peter Falkenberg. And more guns and jewellery from the same robbery had been dug up in the wood at Meererbusch where Boost had been caught.

Franz was arrested. His alibi showed that he was serving a prison term for poaching when the Buderich robbery was carried out. And he was still in jail when Falkenberg and Wassing were killed.

How then, Eynck asked, had he come into possession of the stolen property? Franz admitted that he had been given them by Boost. But he maintained he didn't know they were stolen.

For the first time Eynck had been able to establish a link, admittedly a tenuous one, between Boost and one of the killings: the robbery—the gun—the bullet which killed Falkenberg—the cache in the wood—Franz—and Boost.

Then on December 15th, 1956, came the find which really

assured Boost's guilt. Workers at Buderich cemetery were relaying a hedge. Digging up the old thorn fence they came across a miniature treasure trove—jewellery, gold trinkets, clocks, firearms and other weapons, mainly collectors' pieces. They were wrapped inside a car inner-tube and some bits were inside sealed jars.

A 5.6 mm. pistol was found wrapped inside a page from a newspaper. A crossword had been filled in on one side of the paper. Boost's sister-in-law said she had done a similar crossword at Boost's home. A comparison was made with her handwriting: it was the same as the block-lettering on the newspaper.

Eynck went back to see Mrs. Boost. She said she remembered her husband bringing jewellery home one night in January, 1956. Franz was interviewed again. He had heard Boost say he had a hiding-place in the cemetry.

The police technical laboratories turned to an examination of the jars. They contained a jumble of things, including a piece of rope and a medical syringe.

Under the microscope they found that the rope matched the washing-line used to tie up Fräulein Wassing in the hay stack murders. A minute drop of liquid remained in the bottom of the syringe. Examination showed that it was cyanide.

Next, the 'back-room' men looked at the rubber rings which ran round the lip of the jars to seal them. They corresponded with the ring which had been placed round Wassing's head to prevent the gag from slipping.

The 5.6 mm. gun was also sent to Wiesbaden for examination. Its movement was fractionally to the right when fired but only three matching marks were found on a round discharged from the barrel—insufficient to match it with the bullet taken from Falkenberg. Still, Eynck has no doubts privately that it was the gun which was used to shoot Falkenberg.

Eynck instituted another search of Boost's home. He found more rubber rings, a further length of the same type of rope and another syringe filled with cyanide.

The significance of the cyanide was not yet clear. But Eynck felt that he had enough evidence against Boost now.

Two weeks before Boost was due out of prison at Christmas, 1956, Eynck succeeded in obtaining a holding warrant, detaining him in prison as a prime suspect in the case.

The long-shot had worked. Dr. Wehner had always feared that once Boost was free the police would never again have the chance to prove the crimes against him. But Eynck had beaten him to it, by a matter of days.

.   .   .

After a brief Christmas respite, Eynck returned to his temporary headquarters at Dusseldorf at the beginning of January, 1957, three courses of inquiry charted out in his mind. One way lay through Boost himself: if Boost would not talk something useful might be picked up from a study of his character and life-history seen through the eyes of other people.

The second line of investigation would start with Franz, now being held in custody on suspicion of receiving stolen property. The third depended upon the value of the scientific and general background evidence being amassed at Wiesbaden and by his crime squads.

First Eynck dug into Boost's past. He wanted to know much more about the man he was up against: 'I wanted to get inside his mind and see what made him tick.' Eynck came up with many of the answers; in a way he uncovered more than he reckoned for—Boost's history disclosed links with past crimes in others parts of the country.

Eynck went to the offices of the social welfare authorities responsible for youth work. There he found Boost on the files as a former inmate of a home for delinquents. Boost was the bastard child of a sixteen-year-old country girl who had given the unwanted baby to her mother to bring up.

From the reports, Boost had obviously been a difficult child. A schoolmaster had written: 'He is late each morning. His grandmother says that he prowls around up to the late hours at night. He comes home when everybody is asleep. In the morning she cannot wake him up.

'When his grandmother tried to dress him he used to beat and kick her. I have never met a child so disobedient. He laughs in my face and no punishment can change him. He kicks and fights his fellow pupils. All the children in his neighbourhood are afraid of him. He steals out of other pupils' desks.'

Eynck next turned to Boost's family and friends. He learned that Boost had been brought up in Saxony, an area of Germany split in two at the end of the war by the zones of occupation. At one stage in his youth he had gone to live with a baker and his family to learn the trade. But Boost had got into trouble again and eventually he was taken away and placed in a welfare home. In the last year of the war, at the age of seventeen, he was called up but was soon taken prisoner by the British and later released.

From one relative, Eynck learned that Boost had spent several years at the end of the war in the small town of Haldensleben.

Between 1945 and 1950 he had lived in this small town, thirty miles inside the new East German republic, close to the Helmstedt-Berlin autobahn and had met his wife there. In those years millions of refugees, many Germans among them, were fleeing from the Russian occupying forces and to reach the west had to cross the Iron Curtain which had split Europe down the middle.

Eynck found out that Boost had earned a highly dangerous living at that time as a border guide, illegally escorting parties of refugees across the border into West Germany. He knew every inch of the Saxony countryside and so could avoid the 'man-traps' placed by the Russians, the mine-fields, barbed wire and machine gun emplacements.

But at that time in history the aftermath of war and the suspension of civilised standards had made life for those who remained largely a matter of the survival of the fittest. Between 1945 and 1950 there were about eighty murders in the border zone which could not be attributed to political motives. They were nearly all refugees, shot or strangled and their few possessions stolen in the woods and hills of Saxony as they made the secret journey to what they had hoped would be their 'new life'.

Military law had little time to spare to investigate these crimes: civil law had broken down — the rule of the jungle had returned. More than fifty murders remained unsolved when Eynck set about the task of investigating Boost's past.

One member of Boost's family said that he used to go off for days and returned in a wild dishevelled state, refusing to say where he had been. Although he did not work he had plenty of money and boasted that he had enough riches to last him for life. A woman told Eynck that she remembered Boost often coming to Dusseldorf from the eastern zone to sell clothing and jewels. A baker, now living in Hanover, had recognised Boost's picture in a newspaper as that of the man he had seen committing a robbery murder on the border in 1947.

Another man volunteered the evidence that Boost had told him how he shot down a Red Army soldier during one crossing to the west. From other witnesses Eynck heard of Boost's boast that he had committed a number of robberies and at least one murder. It was indicative of some link that the series of murders had stopped once Boost came to live permanently in Dusseldorf in 1950. By 1951, Boost was in jail, serving a nine month prison sentence for stealing urns off graves to sell to metal dealers.

Boost had had only a primary school education but Eynck learned from his family that he had studied diligently at home, especially applying himself to the basics of chemistry. 'He was a self-taught man and extremely intelligent. He seemed to devote himself to anything that could help in the destruction of life. He knew how to mix and prepare poisons, how to shoot with great accuracy. He was an expert in unarmed combat, he was building two machine guns in the cellar of his home and had somehow got hold of a British-made weapon.'

In all Eynck considers that Boost was 'probably the most dangerous man I have ever met. If his talents had been turned in the right direction he could have been a great asset to society.'

Eynck felt that he now knew something of the calibre of the man he was trying to put permanently behind bars. He next began to develop the theory of the 'two man' crimes. One was the Dr. Servé case. Eynck knew Boost had been free at this time. He sent for the list of all pistols handed to the police in that year. When he came to the 08 weapon which lacked the firing pin he read on the label: 'Unable to test: firing pin is missing.' Eynck cross-checked in the police lost-and-found book to see where and when it had been discovered. When he read the entry 'Found in the Theveser Feld' he felt what he later described as a tingling sensation. The connection was obvious at once: it was Boost's former home address, the prefabricated house he had built for his family when they came to settle in Dusseldorf from the eastern zone.

The pistol was sent to Wiesbaden for testing. The police laboratory sent back a report: 'The marks on the test bullet fitted with which Dr. Servé was killed. The grooves on the inside of the barrel make us certain that the 08 pistol you sent us is the murder weapon.'

Eynck's initial reactions of shock and annoyance have now mellowed with time. He puts the error down to 'a series of human failures. We all make mistakes. The only perfect detective was Sherlock Holmes and he never left the pages of fiction.'

At the time Wiesbaden were examining the gun in February, 1957, Franz fell ill in prison. He called for Eynck who took him back to the murder office with a solicitor. There, Franz said that he wanted to talk or he would go crazy. He said his wife was expecting a child and he wanted 'to clear his conscience' before it was born.

The story Franz told made it clear that he had been under the spell of a maniac. 'He lived in perpetual fear of Boost. For four years he had suffered mental torture because of his knowledge of the crimes he had committed with Boost. He said he had been living on drugs to keep himself going.'

Franz said he had been hypnotised into committing crimes with Boost. 'He told me they had become friends when they

went out shooting game together. Soon Franz became aware of
Boost's obsession with courting couples. He said Boost would
creep upon them and demand money. After robbing the men,
Boost would rape the women and try to persuade his companion to do the same.'

Franz told the detective that Boost had been experimenting
with new ways of killing people. He had prepared a drug
which he would inject into the couple, under threat of shooting,
to stupify them. On the evening of the Servé murder, Boost
had given him some pep pills. Boost had intended to rob the
occupants of the first car they came across and then steal the
car. 'I will never forget the look on Boost's face,' Franz said.
'He was white, his eyes were staring. He looked like a wolf:
I was terrified of him.'

Franz said that after the murder he had run away across the
fields but Boost had caught up with him. Boost had told him to
go back and shoot Servé's companion, Hüllecremer, or he
would be killed. Franz had fallen to his knees promising never
to give Boost away and had sworn an oath not to reveal what
he had seen. Then they had finished the night by sharing the
contents of Servé's wallet.

He told the detective of other meetings he had had with
Boost in the Rotterdamer Strasse. One night when it was cold
and foggy, Franz had waited several hours for Boost to arrive.
When Boost finally turned up there were specks of blood on his
coat. Boost had brought along some toy balloons filled with
cyanide gas. Franz said Boost planned to let the gas out into a
parked car.

Then he intended to attack the occupants when they were
overcome by the gas. That night Boost had returned a gun, a
.38, he had borrowed from Franz. It had not been fired but the
handle was covered in clay.

Re-reading this part of the long confession later, Eynck
sensed it might refer to the night when Behre and Kürmann
had been driven into the gravel tip. Boost had given Franz
fourteen pounds in repayment of a debt—the same sum which
had been stolen from the couple.

Eynck went back and questioned Franz again. He could only recall the date by something which he had read in the paper the next day. Checking back, Eynck turned up the newspaper article and the date—November 1st, 1955. It was the morning after the disappearance of Behre and Kürmann.

There was much more that Franz had to tell of his time spent virtually as a prisoner of Boost. Once Boost had injected him with a 'truth serum' and under the effects of the drug had interrogated him to find out if he would ever talk to the police. Other times he had fed his companion with pep pills which made Franz feel like 'a wild hunter'.

On one occasion they had gone to an isolated villa in the woods outside Dusseldorf to rob and kill the three occupants. But Franz had pretended he could not break into the house and on this pretext had managed to get Boost away.

From what Eynck heard, Boost seemed to live in a fantasy world, planning new ways of committing crime. Most of his plans, fortunately, had remained fantasies. He wanted to raid a post office and planned to fill bottles with gas, deliver them in a parcel to the post office just before closing time, then await developments. A mechanism would open the bottles, the gas would stupify the people inside and he would go in wearing a gas-mask to steal at will.

To attack and rob people in cars, Boost laid planks of wood covered with nails and sharp metal points across a country road. He carried this plan out but none of the cars were ever halted.

Franz told of Boost's experiments with chemicals. He claimed to have been able to produce a poison from a species of wild potato which had the same characteristics as kurari. In the cellar of his home he manufactured liquid cyanide which he meant to inject by means of a syringe into the bodies of men and women and overpower them.

'The syringe we found under the hedge in Buderich cemetery contained traces of cyanide. But we could never prove that he used it. There were no traces found in the bodies.

'Still, this does not exclude its use altogether. The bodies had been badly burned and as cyanide spreads very quickly, after a time all traces vanish.'

The testimony Franz had given was sufficient, taken with the scientific evidence, to crush any defence that Boost could offer. But Eynck still persisted in running confirmatory evidence.

He wanted to pin Boost's ownership to the 08 pistol so that it was beyond any dispute. He learned from Boost's wife that she had seen her husband with an 08 pistol in the summer of 1952 when he was using it for shooting practice. Two other witnesses who had seen the same gun at that time in Boost's house picked out the exact one from a collection of 08 weapons assembled for the purpose by the police.

Then, unexpectedly, evidence arrived from East Germany, strengthening Boost's association with the gun. The public prosecutor of the city of Magdeburg contacted his opposite number in Dusseldorf telling him that Boost was suspected of an attempted murder there on a policeman in 1948—and that the weapon used was an 08 pistol. Also the East Germans said the same gun had been used to shoot and seriously injure a border policeman in the same year. Magdeburg is only about twelve miles from Haldensleben, Boost's home during the first post-war years. But the political situation existing between the two Germanys prevented Boost ever being returned to Madgeburg to answer to any alleged crimes. Whatever the strength of the allegations against Boost for his activities the far side of the Iron Curtain, these have now presumably been written off.

It took Eynck six months to assemble the evidence against Boost and Franz, his fear-stricken accomplice. But in July, 1957 the detective finally handed to the public prosecutor a dossier detailing the strength of the police case. The court trials ran on for another two years until, late in 1959, Boost was found guilty of the five murders and sent to prison for life. To the last, he never admitted his guilt of any of the crimes. Even in prison while awaiting trial, Boost's remarkable self-confidence never let him down. To one of his daughters he sent a drawing of 'Papa' in the shape of a devil, complete with horns and tail.

After the notoriety of the case, his wife divorced him and moved away from her home with the children.

Franz, who had had no part in any of the killings save his eye-witness role in the Dr. Servé murder, was jailed for six years. One of the few happy features for Eynck in the whole case was a visit out of the blue which he received in 1965 from Franz. He had come to express his gratitude for the help the police had given him. 'Today that man has redeemed himself completely. He has found himself a good job and is happily married. He has put Boost behind him.'

No awards were handed out for the policemen in the Boost affair. Too many mistakes had been made before Eynck came on the scene for the public to feel completely happy about the conduct of the Dusseldorf police.

But Eynck's reputation as the master of murder investigation had withstood its supreme test. 'What is probably more important, it eased my way to promotion and gave me more money.'

Eynck's relations with the nieghbouring Dusseldorf detectives are still surprisingly harmonious. 'Neither side ever let the Boost case affect its relationship. I never discuss Boost but that is just my way of being discreet.

'I feel that today at last I can speak quite openly and honestly of the mistakes which were made: *sine ira et studio* (without anger or enthusiasm).'

ROMOLO IMUNDI: AMERICA

The Missing Women Mystery

The Missing Women Mystery

Violent death is no stranger to Romolo J. Imundi, homicide detective first grade.

Among New York's swarming millions he has investigated 500 killings: Mafia executions in central Manhattan, bar brawls in Times Square, psychopathic killers in Harlem.

Imundi, father of four, holds eighteen citations for outstanding work as a civil servant. With over 1,000 arrests to his name, he is still not inured to crime. 'Every case is different. No two homicides are alike: no two approaches by the detective can be the same.'

Twenty-five years' police service have taken Imundi from a patrolman's beat in Harlem to a $14,000 a year job in the homicide division. Yet in all his experience he has never met a case so complex as that of the death of Puerto Rican beauty queen, Pinky Domenech.

The violence of the crime was overshadowed by the intricacies of motive and opportunity which Imundi and fellow detectives from seven countries on both sides of the Altantic had to unwind to find their suspect.

Some murders remain unsolved by a matter of luck or stupidity: in the Domenech case the skill of the killer was matched by the foresight of the police. At times the inquiry resembled a game of chess in which the stake was a man's liberty.

It was one case where Imundi never saw the D.O.A. (police phraseology for a 'Dead on arrival.') Pinky Domenech died 3,000 miles from home beneath the cliffs of a remote Irish beauty resort, her body pounded by the Atlantic breakers.

Apart from woman detective Julia McNamara, assigned from

the New York police department's Missing Persons Bureau, Imundi met none of the other policemen working with him on the case. And yet, as an example of international police co-operation, its like has rarely been seen.

Despite this, in the precise sense the outcome for Imundi and his colleagues was: failure. If detection is a mere matter of 'winning' and 'losing' then nobody won. Imundi did not obtain a conviction or even an admission of guilt: Patrick J. D'Arcy, Pinky Domenech's lover—at forty-five, seventeen years her senior—did not live very long afterwards with the knowledge of the crime the police are satisfied he committed.

D'Arcy killed himself. Thus there was a strange sort of equality between hunter and hunted at the end. Except, that is, for one matter which remains totally unexplained even today—three years later.

This is the disappearance of Pinky's mother, dark-haired, fiery-tempered Mrs. Virginia Domenech, member of a prominent Puerto Rican family. By a quirk of fate it was a report that she was missing that brought the later events to light.

Hundreds of men and women disappear in New York every year. Most turn out to be unfaithful husbands, unstable wives, footloose children or just drop-outs who want to shake the past from their system.

Only a handful of cases filter up from the missing persons bureau to the city's detective departments, mostly because they have an element of suspicious circumstance about them.

When detective Julia McNamara opened the door of Mrs. Virginia Domenech's apartment on the evening of June 2nd, 1967, she found nothing to suggest the violence which had already overtaken the family. The wardrobe was full of clothes, the deep freeze well-stocked with bread, milk and meat. There were scraps of food in the waste bin and letters lying on the living-room table which had been taken in from the mail-box but left unopened.

Everything McNamara found suggested that Mrs. Domenech had left on the spur of the moment and had intended to be away for only a short time. She established that Mrs. Domenech had not been to her office since the previous Wednesday. She worked as an $8,000 a year social worker at the Hebrew Children's Home in the Bronx, across the Harlem river from her home in Washington Heights, Manhattan. It was Mrs. Domenech's employer who had first become worried about her whereabouts.

When Thursday and Friday had passed without any sign of Mrs. Domenech, the supervisor at her office called at the apartment to see what was wrong. She found the flat empty and informed the missing persons bureau.

A purple dress and a pair of green and purple shoes were the only things the police were able to pin-point by their absence from the apartment at 103, Bennett Avenue. Mrs. Domenech had been wearing them when she left work on May 31st.

A check of her movements at work suggested nothing abnormal. It was established that she went straight home from the office. But from the moment she entered the apartment block her life stopped short.

A missing persons bulletin was issued by the police. But there has never been any response: Mrs. Domenech walked into oblivion when she stepped over the threshold of her home that evening in 1967.

Neighbours in the block said she lived with her daughter Maria—nicknamed Pinky—who worked with the New York City Bureau of Child Welfare.

Pinky Domenech too was nowhere to be found. But there was nothing mysterious in that. She was away in Europe on a three-week early summer vacation and would not be home until June 7th. She was travelling around without any forwarding address. As she was expected back in five days' time, the police decided to wait. They confidently expected that she would be able to throw some light on her mother's movements.

In the meantime the Puerto Rican police were asked to find out if Mrs. Domenech had turned up there. Members of the Domenech family in San Juan said they had received holiday messages from Pinky in Europe but nothing was known about her mother.

On Wednesday June 7th, Julia McNamara waited for the word from the customs and immigration department at Kennedy airport that Pinky had arrived back.

She was due in on Pan-Am flight 117 from Paris. But the call never came. The next day, when there was still no news, McNamara reported the facts to her chief at the missing persons bureau.

Taking the cases in isolation there was nothing at this stage to set them out from a hundred and one other disappearing men and women. Mrs. Domenech might be ill, suffering from amnesia or the victim of an accident, unable to identify herself.

As for Pinky, it was then the height of the Middle East crisis which had developed into the Six Day War and she might be having difficulty in getting on to a flight with American tourists flocking back home in their thousands to avoid involvement in the shooting match. Or she might have decided to extend her holiday in Europe by a few days.

But reading the two cases together, then McNamara felt the situation was capable of a more sinister interpretation, though it was impossible as yet even to guess at what that was.

The file went from missing persons to Lieutenant Sullivan of the New York police department. He agreed to detach to it one of his detectives, 'Ronnie' Imundi, a member of the Manhattan North Homicide Squad in whose area the Domenechs had lived.

. . .

As a member of the world's busiest homicide squad, Imundi— pronounced I-Mundi—is virtually three people rolled into one. There is the detective, the man who can never afford to be without his ·38 detective special automatic; there is Imundi the vice-president of his detectives' 'union' and there is Imundi the private citizen, spending his free time and money 'to give a break to less fortunate kids.'

As negotiator for the 3,500 members of the New York detective endowment association Imundi was instrumental in winning a £2,000,000 increase in salaries and fringe benefit for his colleagues.

In his twenty-six years as a policeman Imundi has won eighteen citations for outstanding work as a civil servant. A model citizen, he is a member of the Holy Rosary building fund and organises buses free of charge to take children from the New York slums to summertime holiday camps.

Imundi is as proud and loquacious about New York as he is dedicated to his job. 'This city is a tremendous challenge for the policeman—100 different nationalities. The versatility of the American detective is tremendous: it has to be. I speak four languages: you got to be ready to diversify your abilities. One day you're talking to a professor at Columbia University: the next a shoe-shine boy, a hustler.'

Because of his Italian background, Imundi has been specially employed on Mafia crimes. He was assigned to the Park Sheraton Hotel barber's shop shooting of Albert Anastasia, head of Murder Inc., the attempt to kill Frank Costello outside his apartment block on Central Park West and, more recently, the Senate crime commission hearings into the revelations of Joseph Valachi.

Imundi also worked on the George Metesky 'Mad Bomber of Manhattan' case; the torso killing of Jackie Smith; 'hitman' Elmer Burke, suspected of seven murders for payment, executed for one, and compulsive slayer Joe Donohue, now serving thirty-five years to life in Sing Sing.

In what is essentially a sordid job, the detective must guard against becoming warped by the section of humanity he meets. Imundi, working so close to such sub-human behaviour, nevertheless manages to retain a high degree of urbanity.

There is little of the violence about him that one might expect from his upbringing as a member of an ethnic minority group. 'I was a blockbuster. When I was seven my father, an Italian Catholic, moved the family into a part of New York populated by Irish, German and English immigrants.

'I was the first "guinea" (slang for Italian) in the block. The other kids gave me hell. They used to burn my school books,

break my windows. Once they lay in waiting for me on my way
home from school. They tore the clothes off my back, tarred and
feathered me and wrote "Guinea Eats Shit" on my backside.'

Yet despite the violence which permeates his working life,
Imundi personally would favour the banning of firearms in
America. 'But as things stand, it would be suicidal for the
police to be unarmed. The gun is the great equaliser: when
you're standing behind it you're big: when you're in front of it
you're two foot tall.'

But there is much more to being a good detective than a
tough exterior and a quick trigger-finger. Though Imundi was
not to know it when the double missing persons file was
handed to him, it was a case which was to exercise to the full all
his powers of deduction and interrogation as an investigator.

First he and Julia McNamara built up a pen picture of each
woman:

Virginia Domenech, aged fifty-two, divorced from her
husband Fernando in 1946. He was an accountant in San Juan,
her brother, Rafael Angel Rivera Cruz, a Justice Department
lawyer in Puerto Rico. She had been living in New York since
the marriage broke down, an intelligent, personable woman who
had become completely Americanised over the passing years.

Maria Virginia Domenech, aged twenty-eight, one of three
children. Called Pinky by her friends because of her petite
(five feet two inches) beauty. Her home had broken up when
she was seven years old. She stayed on in Puerto Rico, living
with her father until she was fifteen, then went to live with her
mother. College education; won a beauty contest in 1963 and
went on a month-long visit to Italy as the first prize. The
following year she got a job with the Spanish Iberian Airways,
then took up a job among socially inadequate children — the
work for which her psychology degree had prepared her.

Imundi dug more deeply into the background of both women,
seeking an answer in their pasts for their disappearance. 'Both
had first-class characters: our investigations turned up nothing
but favourable information.'

He found that neither had money worries — apart from their

combined salaries of £6,000 a year, both had private incomes derived from family settlements. There was not breath of scandal surrounding their home lives—Pinky was known to have a number of boyfriends but to Imundi, himself the father of a twenty-year-old daughter, there would have been more ground for suspicion if there had been no men in the girl's life.

Imundi and Julia McNamara went back to the apartment in Bennett Avenue and systematically took it apart. 'It was very orderly, very neat. How much clothing was missing—if any—was hard to ascertain because there was so much. As we pulled the closets apart they were full of clothes.'

It was in the detectives' mind that Mrs. Domenech might have gone to Europe to join her daughter. 'If that was in her mind—and all the clothes she had left behind, not to mention her passport, made it highly unlikely—she was bound to have told the superintendent of the apartment block.'

One of the cardinal rules of the detective on an inquiry is: always tell outsiders as little as possible. It prevents witnesses from unconsciously colouring their testimony with facts the policeman has told them; it prevents them embroidering the truth with possibly disastrous consequences later in court and it enables the investigator to obtain completely unadulterated evidence.

For Imundi there is another angle too. 'When you go to see the superintendent—or anybody else—you have to impress upon them that this is just a routine inquiry. If you let them know the full implications of the case they may clam up on you and you lose their confidence.'

Obeying this rule rewarded Imundi with one small but significant piece of information. The superintendent of the block said it was odd for mother and daughter both to be away at the same time. It was also usual for each woman to tell the superintendent when they were coming back. On this occasion they had told her nothing.

To Imundi the case was fast assuming homicide status. 'At each plateau, as the questions we asked went unanswered, Julia and I became more concerned.'

But with no body and no hard evidence of murder it was going to be a question of starting at Z and working backwards through to A.

.   .   .

When a policeman is up against a blank wall, his training teaches him that there is only one way out: start asking the same questions of the same people all over again in the hope of seeing something in a different light.

Despite all available evidence to the contrary, Imundi reasoned that previous events must have some connection with the disappearance of both women. Of the two, a further examination of Pinky's life offered the more probable hope of reward. Her age and personality suggested that she had more outside points of contact than her mother.

'We started to go more deeply this time into Pinky's boy-friends, her colleagues at the office, her diary. We started asking the people at her office who she went with. We turned up the names of several boyfriends and began to check them all out.'

Asking questions of a personal nature demands a certain delicate skill if the interviewee is going to tell the truth. 'There's a certain amount of embarrassment in it for the boy. It's got to be a soft sell. You have to watch his reaction at the mention of Pinky's name. Everything he says must be checked out even though he doesn't know it.'

Each boy was gently quizzed about his dates with Pinky, how often they went out, where, how far the friendship went.

'You have to play it by ear. There are no books which tell you how to handle this kind of situation. Here, the ex-pertise of the individual comes into its own.

'Take for example the time when I have to go and interview a guy in his office about his girlfriend. First I've got to get past the secretary—without telling her what I'm about, naturally. It's no use just flashing your badge and trying the heavy-handed approach. That will put the man on his guard straight-away.

'When I'm inside his office I reckon I've got fifteen seconds to get him interested enough to discuss matters with me. If that guy feels you are talking about a homicide case, well, you're blown.'

For the first time the name of Patrick D'Arcy entered the inquiry. Pinky had mentioned him in office gossip as a friend who worked in the travel agency business in Manhattan.

At this stage, D'Arcy was just one name on the list of men who had been attracted by Pinky's flashing smile, her quiet, tranquil personality and her impeccable taste in good, expensive clothes.

But the visits by the detectives to the child welfare bureau, their persistent questioning, began to stir memories. Bits and pieces of evidence that normally would have had no significance at all began to break the surface of the case.

From one of Pinky's colleagues, Imundi learned that she had confided before she went on holiday that she might be meeting D'Arcy in Rome, and might even settle down there with him.

Imundi checked the girl's bank account and found that she had withdrawn £2,500—all her savings—from two bank accounts. She had even raised a loan of £650 from a third bank saying she wanted to invest it in a business venture.

These facts indicated for the first time that Pinky may never have intended to return home. If she had settled down in a new life in Europe—as she was quite free to do—this might have precipitated her mother's departure. But where?

But if Pinky intended to stay in Europe there was one known fact which did not fit in to the picture. She had bought a return air ticket. Perhaps, Imundi reasoned, it was something to fall back on if Pinky's plans crumbled.

Pursuing each angle, Imundi wondered if the return ticket meant that Pinky was not completely certain of D'Arcy. With each question he asked, D'Arcy's name was coming up positive in the answer.

It was a question now of when to interview the man. With none of the facts, let alone the 'aces', in his hand Imundi felt it might be better to wait until the police knew exactly the extent of the inquiry.

For the moment there was just one other fact to be added to the very sparse dossier. A friend of the Domenech family said he had taken Pinky to Kennedy airport on May 17th. Mrs. Domenech had gone too and they had seen the girl board Pan-Am flight 110 leaving at eighteen-thirty, bound for Rome. Pinky had left alone, there was no doubt of this. Mrs. Domenech had returned to the apartment afterwards.

The New York police began to go through points of routine procedure which might help to sharpen the case.

All unidentified female bodies in the New York morgues had to be checked. It was Julia McNamara's grizzly but necessary job to keep tabs on all D.O.A. reports. Every time one turned up on the slab—the victim of a road accident or a river drowning—and there was no identification apart from the tag 'Female White Unknown' McNamara would call up Imundi and together they would visit the morgue. 'But it was never one of ours.'

Fingerprints of the Domenechs were available from the record cards held by the women's employers, the New York city authorities. Getting details of their dentures was not so easy—yet apart from fingerprints they are the body's most telling feature of identification to detectives.

'We eventually tracked down a dentist who had treated Pinky. He told us he had done a very expensive job capping her teeth,' said Imundi. 'You would be surprised how often teeth identification helps. We've had skeletons that have come to light after three or four years. We tackle the jaw back to the dentist and he is able to tell us with certainty that he has worked on that person.'

Both sets of fingerprints and dental charts were sent to the Federal Bureau of Investigation's identification division in Washington where they took their place among 200,000,000 such print records.

At the request of the New York police the F.B.I. circulated the details to the Interpol offices at St. Cloud on the outskirts of

Paris. With Pinky positively placed in Europe the answer might lie on the other side of the Atlantic.

It was just routine police procedure. But all the same it blew the investigation wide open. Unknown to Imundi and McNamara another police force 3,000 miles away had its hands full of a mystery which was to unite the two bureaux in one baffling murder.

．　　．　　．

On May 24th, 1967—nine days before the New York police entered the case—the body of a girl, wearing only black panties, was washed ashore on the Irish coast a couple of miles down water from the Cliffs of Moher, a remote beauty spot on the Atlantic shoreline in Co. Clare. She was found lying wedged between rocks on Doolin Strand, a stretch of sand eight miles from the nearest town, Lisdoonvarna—a famous spa resort.

The Cliffs of Moher are one of the major tourist attractions along Ireland's west coast, a magnet for summer-time visitors from America and continental Europe. They are five miles in length and fall in a sheer precipice 668 feet down to the Atlantic below.

Doolin Strand lies beneath the shadow of Moher, across a narrow treacherous corner of the ocean. On the flat heath at the top of the cliffs is O'Brien's Tower, a 150-years-old castled folly, round whose base swirl the gales blowing in from the sea.

The body was found early that morning by a fisherman wandering across Doolin beach. Police carried the body to a lifeboat house pending identification and a pathologist arrived to carry out a post-mortem examination.

It seemed unlikely that there would be much difficulty in finding out who the girl was. From the state of the body it was obvious she had not been in the water more than a day when she was found. The panties bore an American trade-mark widely sold in multiple stores which made a single purchase impossible to check.

The pathologist, Dr. Maurice Hickey, found that the woman's spine and most of her ribs were fractured and the liver lacerated. There was no evidence to show she had been raped. She had probably fallen from a height but it was not possible to tell whether the injuries had occurred before or during the fall.

A study of tidal conditions in the area proved beyond doubt that for the girl to have been washed up at this point she must have entered the water at a spot directly underneath the Cliffs of Moher. There had been previous cases of accidental drowning where people had fallen off the cliffs. But this could not have been the answer to the tragedy of the girl in black briefs: there was no sign of her clothes.

A search of the flat land at the top of the cliffs revealed a bloodstained gold bracelet. This was taken away for fingerprint tests, but without result.

The American briefs suggested a girl tourist. It was early yet for the annual invasion of Co. Clare by holiday-makers and a check of hotels and boarding-houses in and around Lisdoonvarna produced only one girl who might fit the description of the dead person on Doolin beach.

She was an American, aged around thirty, and her name was Patricia H. Kelly, a hospital receptionist from San Diego, California. Miss Kelly who was on a tour of the British Isles had left the area a few days before. When inquiries in surrounding areas of Ireland failed to place her whereabouts, the body was tentatively given Miss Kelly's name.

The inquest at Ennis on May 25th was well under way when Police Superintendent John Butler announced to the coroner, Dr. J. C. Counihan, that Miss Kelly had been discovered alive and well in Aberdeen.

The inquest broke up in uproar. The police double-checked this information. Miss Kelly did resemble the dead girl but she had been traced by a forwarding address she had left in Lisdoonvarna.

When the inquest was resumed at Ennis later in the summer, the verdict of the jury was that the girl 'died as a result of multiple injuries by falling from a height'. The coroner held that there was no evidence to show how she had died.

On June 1st, the unknown girl's body, contained in a plain white coffin, was lowered into a grave at Drumcliffe cemetery, Ennis, The record of the burial reads simply: 'Grave No. 308, Plot No. 9.'

In Dublin, 150 miles away, two members of the technical bureau—Ireland's Murder Squad—Detective Inspector Bernard Moore and Detective Sergeant John Courtney were given the job of identifying the girl and finding out how she died.

They checked with ships to see if there were any reports of a woman being lost overboard. At one time there was a theory that she might have fallen into the sea from an aircraft or even a helicopter. But neither idea turned up any results. The detectives were certain that the girl was a foreigner—apart from the panties she had swarthy features that marked her out from the fresh-complexioned Irish womenfolk.

Again as a matter of routine the Irish murder squad detectives decided to send her fingerprints to Interpol and the F.B.I. The body had not been in the water long enough for decomposition to have set in so Detective Sergeant William Byrne of the Dublin technical bureau was able to scrape the skin from the tips of the fingers to get impressions. Along with the fingerprints went details of the girl's dentures—an expensive capping job on a number of the upper teeth.

In Washington, a clerk in the F.B.I. identifications division ran out a check on the details supplied by the Irish police. Within a few minutes he had found a card to match them. The card related to one Maria Virginia Domenech, aged twenty-eight, a girl reported missing from her apartment in New York City since June 7th.

.   .   .

It was mid-August—high summer—in New York when Ronnie Imundi received the message from Washington that Pinky Domenech had turned up—dead—in Ireland. Ten weeks had gone by, seventy days in which Imundi felt that he knew a lot about the Domenech women but nothing at all of their deaths; which was his job.

In this time, Imundi had got to know Patrick D'Arcy, meeting him first by invitation at the police station, then at D'Arcy's home.

Imundi had gone about meeting his man in a ploy to keep the temperature cool. 'The first time out, I rang him at his office and told him I wanted to see him.'

D'Arcy's response to the phone call was to ask why—then when. 'I said "Take your time. Come on down to my office at your convenience." I didn't want to discuss it on the telephone.'

This, to Imundi, is one of the little points of the skilled detective. 'By calling him on the telephone it disarms the man completely. He assumes: "Gee, homicide guy calling on the phone, he mustn't be too clever."

'But actually you are being very sharp, getting him to drop his guard.

'It is so important to make him think that you don't know anything. You impress him with being too sharp or too wily and up goes that barrier.'

Imundi is acutely conscious of the diplomacy that is required when meeting and questioning a person from a different background. 'I happened to be an American of Italian extraction going against an American of Irish extraction. So, in any dialogue you must make that man feel you aren't too sharp. All the time you've got to be casual—even when you're bursting to ask the vital question.'

So, after the line had been baited by the friendly telephone call, D'Arcy took a cab to the West 100th street precinct station: the notice on its front window announcing 'Spanish Spoken Here.'

On the fourth floor Imundi sat him in the bleak interview room with its flickering neon light and the one-way mirror through which a detective can observe, undetected, from the next room.

Imundi had done some preliminary work on D'Arcy's background prior to this first meeting. He knew the man was married and had two children, one, Evan, aged twelve, a polio victim.

He knew too that D'Arcy was in the holiday business, vice-president of a large travel agency off Fifth Avenue, Manhattan.

D'Arcy turned out to be a giant of a man physically, six feet two inches, florid-faced, ruggedly handsome, immensely amiable and possessed of a good line of 'patter'. His forbears were Irish and D'Arcy had retained much of the whimsical humour of the old country.

At the time of that first meeting, D'Arcy was just another name on the list of Pinky's boyfriends. Detectives must always guard against reading too much into a suspicious situation: 'Maybe it is happening but you have got to prove it' is the dictat with which Imundi disciplines himself.

'You must assume that we all have the motive and that we all have the skeleton in the closet. I may not hit pay dirt on what I am looking for. But I may always turn up evidence in another case.'

(In the Mad Bomber inquiry, Imundi and his fellow detectives ran down leads that brought arrests in a number of completely unrelated crimes. 'You might pick up a fellow on a charge of robbery or grand larceny leading out of your work on the bomb case. But the bombings continued so it could not be that individual.')

Imundi's first meeting with D'Arcy was very formal. 'At no time did I let him know what I was checking out. I was just trying to get some daylight. Did he know Pinky? Had he seen her? Had he been with her?'

Imundi already knew the answers — or part of the answers — to these questions. He was testing D'Arcy. An obvious lie, and the man would take on a new importance in the inquiry.

But D'Arcy was straightforward. 'Yes, he said, he did know her and had been out with her — but not since the middle of May.

'Now he's a married man. In this kind of situation I have to let them know I'm not there to go into their morals. I'm just a homicide man.

'You adopt the nonchalant approach: men are men. I've been all over the world. I wasn't born a policeman. I was born a man. I only became a policeman because of something I liked. But underneath my uniform is a man.

'I have the same likes, I cry, I bleed, I hate, I love. We all have the frailties and vicissitudes of life and when you approach it that way the other fellow realises you are no different.

'Once a detective gains the confidence of an individual and doesn't try to embarrass or hurt him, that man begins to accept what you are saying.'

D'Arcy told Imundi that he had had a platonic friendship with Pinky. Then he said something that surprised the detective: 'he told us he knew Mrs. Domenech well and had been at their apartment a number of times.'

This was news to the police. If they had discovered it from a third person it might have been damaging for D'Arcy. Coming from his lips it suggested either frankness and an untroubled conscience—or a clever man trying to cover his tracks.

After the second interview, Imundi and Julia McNamara sat down in the police station to review what D'Arcy had told them. He admitted giving Pinky a brochure from his travel agency for the tour of Europe. The week before she had left he had suggested places she ought to see. He implied to Pinky that he might fly over himself and meet her there. 'This was all what we call the avenue of constant association.'

But D'Arcy said he had changed his mind and not gone to Europe. He showed Imundi his passport. It was filled with entry and exit stamps—but not between the vital dates when Pinky had taken her holiday. And again he had stressed that he and Pinky had only been casual acquaintances. Nothing could shake him on that point.

While the detectives were considering their next step, the news of the discovery of Pinky's dead body in Ireland reached them.

This information utterly changed what had been until now an essentially local police operation in New York and Eire. Imundi and the Irish murder squad now became the twin hubs of the inquiry with, on the periphery, the forces of France, Germany, Italy and, in Britain, Scotland Yard, working under the aegis of Interpol to try to establish Pinky's movements in Europe.

One dead girl in Ireland, one missing woman — where? America? Despite the lack of personal contact, policemen of half a dozen different tongues combined to make this case a text-book example of international harmony.

.   .   .

The jet-age criminal. In a prophetic speech to leading British policemen in 1967, M. Jean Nepote, the widely-respected secretary general of Interpol, took a glimpse at the future pattern of crime.

He projected the idea of a man who could carry out a crime in London at breakfast time and be in New York by mid-afternoon.

For Ronnie Imundi, the nightmare of keeping hooks on such a man was already a reality. Here was a girl, Pinky Domenech, in Ireland — murdered. There could be no doubt of that. The Irish police had told him their surmise of the incidents at the top of the Cliffs of Moher: attacked, beaten unconscious, stripped to prevent recognition and then hurled into the sea — a brutal, savage killing, the work of a physically strong and probably psychopathic male.

And here in front of him was Patrick D'Arcy — a suspect with an iron-clad alibi to show that he had been 3,000 miles away when the murder took place. Small facts — capable of simple explanation if taken in isolation — were accumulating in a way that made D'Arcy a material witness.

The police could find no business associates who had seen D'Arcy in New York between May 16th and May 26th.

From gossip among Pinky's friends, Imundi knew too that she and D'Arcy had been lovers — not just the hand-across-the-table friends he had made them out to be.

He also learned that the Domenech women had lent D'Arcy

altogether about £4,000, none of which had been repaid. According to the source of this information, Mrs. Domenech had been pressing for the return of her share—and had become more and more acrimonious towards D'Arcy.

Imundi knew the real story of his relationship with Pinky. But why had the mother been persuaded to part with money as well? It was possible—but never in any way proved—that the travel agent had been having some sort of affair with Mrs. Domenech too.

But there was no doubt that from the testimony of neighbours Mrs. Domenech had turned against D'Arcy. And it had happened in the past year. There was a story that he had once attacked Pinky when they were on holiday together. At any rate Mrs. Domenech, suspecting that the couple were lovers, had warned her daughter against this married man—without any success.

But it was all very well for Imundi to build up a wall of suspicion to surround D'Arcy. 'If we couldn't establish that he had been out of America and in Ireland between May 17th and May 24th we were D.O.A. ourselves.'

The detectives were striving to pin on their man what the police academy calls 'exclusive opportunity'—the opportunity of having committed the crime.

More 'straws in the wind' came blowing towards the detectives. D'Arcy's Irish background, the fact that he often went there on business (his passport showed he had been there at least six times in the previous eighteen months), his business associates in Ireland, his admission that he knew the country intimately. But it all meant nothing without the factor of opportunity.

Despite the evidence of the passport, Imundi decided that D'Arcy might have somehow slipped out of the country undetected during the crucial week. With Julia McNamara he began the time-consuming job of checking all flights out of America to Europe in the week following May 16th—D'Arcy's last positive sighting in New York.

They, of course, were looking for the name D'Arcy. Flight

manifests bearing the names of 30,000 passengers who had flown west to east across the Atlantic during the third week of May, 1967, were played onto a viewing screen for the audience of two. The lists, microfilmed so they would fit onto the screen, covered not only Kennedy, but O'Hare, Dulles, San Francisco, in fact every airport which served the trans-Atlantic routes.

'We found several D'Arcy's but none of them fitted our man. They were all too young or too old. The job was driving us crazy but we were still suspicious and determined to come up with an answer. If it cleared D'Arcy, that would be an end to the matter.

'We started figuring another angle: maybe we couldn't get him going out through America, maybe he went out via Canada or Puerto Rico. We checked with the police in each country. Still no luck.'

Imundi and McNamara were running up against a stone wall: 'we just couldn't get him out of the country.' But they kept going, fed on snippets of information from the European police forces which suggested D'Arcy *had* swum through the net despite the evidence to the contrary before their eyes on the screen.

Imundi reasoned that the mistake they were making was in looking for the wrong name: that D'Arcy could have used an alias. Once more they took the 30,000 names and checked them against records of recent issues of passports hoping to match one card with the photograph and personal biography of D'Arcy.

But first the detectives set to work to reduce the 30,000 to a workable size. They went through the names, crossing out women, children, dignitaries and foreigners and then dividing those that remained into D'Arcy's age bracket: between thirty-five and fifty-five to embrace all possibilities.

Half-way through the list they came across the passport issued in New York a few weeks before to an Alfred R. Young. The picture was that of a man with a moustache and glasses. But the accompanying descriptive detail—height six feet two inches, aged forty-five—suggested somebody else to Imundi.

The records showed that Alfred Raymond Young had flown to Rome on May 17th—the same destination, on the same day as Pinky. But he had gone by a later Alitalia flight.

The passport issued to Mr. Young showed a New York address. But when police went to the address they found that Mr. Young was now living at Miami Beach in Florida and had not left there for several months, certainly not to go abroad. Neither had he recently obtained a new passport.

To make quite sure, Imundi had the Florida police send a picture of this Alfred Raymond Young. It wasn't the man in the passport photograph. There was little doubt now that the Alfred Young on the passport was in fact Patrick D'Arcy. Persistence, an instinct for the chase and an ability to put themselves into the mind of the criminal—to be able to predict what he had done—had rewarded the New York detectives.

.   .   .

The trail which once had threatened dismally to peter out now sprang to life in the 'eternal city'. The Rome police traced Pinky to a hotel where she had stayed one night, May 18th. She moved on the next morning and did not turn up again until Naples on May 21st where she was found to have taken a flight to Orly Airport, Paris. But there was no trace at all of D'Arcy in Italy.

In Paris, the French police established that Pinky booked into a hotel on the night of May 21st. The hotel receptionist recalled a man coming to see Pinky that evening. The description certainly fitted D'Arcy: above six feet tall, speaking with a 'trans-Atlantic accent' and wearing American-style clothes. They seemed to be very friendly, the receptionist said. Pinky did not appear to be surprised to see him.

It was nothing positive, but to Imundi 'again one of the small insignificant points that form the overall pattern'.

The following morning, Pinky got up early, breakfasted, then went down to the hotel reception desk and told the clerk that she had changed her plans. Instead of staying in Paris for a week as she had originally intended, she said she wanted to cancel the room.

Pinky checked out at about ten a.m. and was collected in a car by the man who had met her the previous evening.

The car, which had been hired by a Mr. Alfred Young holding a New York driving licence, turned up an hour later at Orly Airport. There, Pinky sent a number of conventional holiday postcards bearing land-marks of Paris while she waited for the plane to carry her to her next destination— London.

Two cards went to her father and uncle in Puerto Rico. One was sent to her mother: 'Europe is prettier than ever. I am having a wonderful time. In a few minutes I am leaving for London. Will be writing in a few days. Love.'

Another card went to her brother Fernando, a student at Cornell University, New York. 'As you can see I am in France. I will send you a sweater from Ireland. I leave today for London.'

What the postcards did not say was more important to the detectives than what they did say. None mentioned the fact that Patrick D'Arcy was now with her.

But this may have been just to avoid stirring up trouble at home. No trace was ever found of the letter she promised her mother. If it was sent, it disappeared with Mrs. Domenech when she walked out of her home for the last time.

When Pinky left Paris that afternoon with D'Arcy she was still travelling under her own name, Maria Domenech. But during the afternoon of May 22nd, while at Heathrow Airport, London, she became Miss M. Young, adopting the alias of her travelling companion.

Scotland Yard found that Pinky had booked ahead—in her own name—to stay in a London West End hotel, but never turned up there. The detectives discovered too that she had cashed $1,000 worth of traveller's cheques at one of the banks in the airport building. Pinky's possession of the cheques was one more link in the chain of evidence connecting her to D'Arcy. They were drawn on the travel agency of which he was

a vice-president but there was no record of Pinky having bought
them in the first place.

Other scraps of detail uncovered by Scotland Yard led to the
conclusion that the change of identity at London was part of a
plan to cover up the couple's trail.

They booked seats in the name of Miss M. Young and Alfred
Young. And they flew to Dublin that evening on separate
flights, Pinky going first and D'Arcy following a couple of
hours later.

There was no apparent reason why the couple should not
have flown together. A check of the plane services that day
showed that they were little more than half-full. It could only
mean that by now there was a deliberate plan afoot.

Pinky may have been led to believe by D'Arcy that this was
part of a scheme to escape to a new life where they could never
be found. But above this speculation flits the thought that
D'Arcy already had murder in mind.

.   .   .

At some time between eleven o'clock and midnight that
night—the last for Pinky—an Alfred R. Young, giving an
address at 244, Riverside Drive, New York, and showing a New
York driving licence, hired a car at Dublin airport.

The Irish police were able to find that the car was returned
nineteen hours later, on the evening of Tuesday, May 23rd.
It had covered about 400 miles in the preceding hours.

With some degree of accuracy, the Dublin murder squad was
able to trace the movements of the car and its occupants
during the crucial time.

At about four-thirty a.m. on May 23rd, a car was noticed
close to the clifftop at Moher. Cars are an infrequent sight at
this spot at any time because there is only a rough track down
to the edge. At that time of the morning it was so unusual as to
stick in the memory of the woman who spotted it from her
lonely farmhouse.

It was near the spot where the car had parked that the

bracelet—bloodstained and belonging to Pinky—was later discovered.

The Cliffs of Moher are about 160 miles from Dublin and a car leaving the capital at around midnight could do the journey in under five hours on deserted roads if the driver was familiar with the route. D'Arcy knew the west coast of Ireland intimately, having relatives and business associates in Galway.

The car—with D'Arcy but no companion—turned up again at eight o'clock that morning some forty miles away. An Alfred Young booked into the International Hotel at Shannon Airport.

It takes about an hour and a half to drive from the Cliffs of Moher to Shannon. So, if the car on the cliff top was D'Arcy's, there is a gap of at least ninety minutes in his movements. That would have been enough for him to have got rid of Pinky's clothing—possibly by burning or burying them in some inaccessible spot—before arriving at Shannon.

Although there is no direct evidence, D'Arcy may have gone to Shannon to try to get onto a direct flight back to America. He probably used the room at the hotel to clean off the marks of any struggle.

But there is an alternative explanation for his movements. Not knowing how soon it would be before Pinky's body was recovered from its watery grave, D'Arcy may have wanted to cover his escape by giving the impression he had flown out of Shannon. When in reality he was doubling back to Dublin.

In fact the body was found by nine o'clock that morning. If the police had had the gift of divination they could have found their chief suspect only forty miles down the road!

Alfred Young checked out of the hotel at midday. He returned his car to the Dublin offices of the hire firm at six-thirty that night, and boarded a plane at eight o'clock the same evening for London.

In London it was established that he flew to Paris the same night—but there all trace of Alfred Young, or Patrick D'Arcy, stopped.

But it is known that he was at Orly Airport long enough to check in two large suitcases at the left luggage bureau—two lady's travelling cases. The French police found them, and inside the wardrobe of the typical American woman tourist — with tabs bearing the name 'Maria Domenech'.

.   .   .

For Imundi, piecing together the mass of fact gathered by his brother detectives on the other side of the Atlantic, 'the answers were at last coming up positive.' D'Arcy had told a series of lies which justified a more direct approach by the detective.

But Imundi was still in a delicate situation. Pinky's death was outside his jurisdiction and he was merely acting as agent for the Irish police who had to take the big decisions in the case. His only personal interest in D'Arcy and the murder was the strength of its connection with Mrs. Domenech's disappearance.

So, as the Irish police probed deeper to dredge up incontrovertible proof, Imundi continued his verbal duels with the travel agent. 'I had a lot on him, a lot more than he thought. I would pinpoint odd facts: "where were you working on such-and-such a night? what did you have to eat that night?" Back would come the answers and I knew that he was lying.'

The relationship between detective and quarry at this time must have been that of a cat with a trapped mouse: Imundi listening, silently noting the discrepancies, D'Arcy holding back the secrets he held of Pinky's last hours alive.

If Imundi had had sole charge of the case — if the killing had taken place within the area of his legal powers — he would have been justified long before in detaining D'Arcy as a material witness.

As it was he was bound to rely on the art of passive interrogation. He gave D'Arcy enough rope with which to hang himself twice over. And the travel agent, though he hid behind a façade of blustering, hearty talk, was slowly being driven towards a mental crack-up.

In the beginning the two men had been amiable and friendly

towards one another. They conducted their meetings as if it was part of a lengthy business negotiation, not an attempt by one to rob the other of his life's freedom.

'But as the discrepancies rolled in, the avenue of interrogation switched from the exploratory to the definite. D'Arcy became antagonistic towards me. He got the feeling with my repeated questions that I was on his back.'

By now D'Arcy's wife was well aware of the importance the detective was assuming in her husband's life though Imundi gave her no inkling what it was about. 'She was getting suspicious of some of her husband's actions and his account of his movements on various days.'

To understand Imundi's approach to the chief—and only—suspect in the Domenech case, it is important to know the man himself. He carries into his work a heavy sense of moral right and wrong. For him crime is a personal matter: he carries a cross for the aggrieved victim, he mourns for the waywardness of the criminal.

'The most gratifying thing in the world is when you are able, deep down in your own heart, to get a man that's killed a stranger to you. I come on the scene, a person is D.O.A. He or she could be white, black, yellow or the red race. I take it on myself to get the individual that has snuffed out this person's life.

'You know, there is nobody who is going to help this poor unfortunate except the homicide detective. You take up the challenge. You're going against a man who thinks he has beaten the system. Then along comes little Ronnie Imundi whom this guy could buy out four times over and nails him.'

But Imundi extends compassion to the criminal as well. As state witness in the case of Elmer 'Trigger' Burke, electrocuted in Sing Sing for murder, Imundi steeled himself to watch the execution 'so I would be fully aware of the implications of my job; so I would be 110 per cent sure next time not to colour my testimony in a homicide case.'

At night, Imundi often takes the job with him to his wife and family in the Bronx. 'You sit and watch the television and

starting an inquisition in your mind: "Gees, I hope I'm right."
Because you do have a conscience, you believe in religion and
in God and you're a family man. Then you get into bed and
you lie there wondering if you should give the guy the benefit
of the doubt.'

In the Domenech case, both men were of the same faith, both
devout Roman Catholics, D'Arcy a loving father who had
taken his lame child to Rome where they had both been received in general audience by Pope Paul.

Imundi's religious beliefs play an important part in his work.
'It makes you more courageous. It's a funny thing to say
but you're in a state of grace and it's nice to know you're
on His side. Religion helps you in many ways. The person— the
D.O.A.—that you are helping is a human being with a soul
and if it isn't for you, who's going to take care of this poor
unfortunate?

'It's just as easy to step away from the responsibility. There's
a lot of people don't give a goshdarn—someone's killed, the
next day they're reading the stock market report.'

To Imundi, every criminal has a chink in his mental armour:
'You find individuals who will confess to you if you reach the
plateau of their religion.

'They all have a weakness—they may be proud or vain,
love their mother, son, daughter or their religion. You've got to
touch that soft underbelly of the man's personality.

'We've had some real tough killers, the kind of feller who
would make your hair stand on end. But they may love their
mother or you may bring their daughter in to see them.
You don't treat him like an animal, you treat him like a
man.'

.   .   .

Timing was now the key to Imundi's next move—choosing
the psychological moment when he might be able to break the
big man.

'We didn't want to be premature. It's very dangerous to

move in too quickly because then you chance losing what you have built up so carefully over the previous months.

'If the Irish police came over or I went to Europe and D'Arcy got to hear of this he might all of a sudden take fright. You get to the stage in this job where you become frustrated in your mind: waiting for the right moment you could scream.'

In the end, D'Arcy did break. But it was in a way that took everybody by surprise.

By the first week in October, everything that could be found to connect D'Arcy with Pinky on her European holiday had been turned up. For Imundi the picture at last began to formulate right before his eyes. 'I decided to go down and get him right there in his house, go right into his bailiwick and confront him.'

There was a dual purpose in this move. One, a confrontation with D'Arcy, pointing out where he had lied, might jerk a confession from him. Two, D'Arcy's wife would be present and might aid the detective to obtain the break-through. 'D'Arcy would have to make one of two moves. He could admit it, or he could lie. Either way, his wife would know now what was going on.'

For Imundi it was a distasteful but necessary move: using a close relative for the purpose of discrediting a suspect and driving a wedge between them.

But when Imundi arrived at the house on October 10th, 1967, Mrs. D'Arcy told him that her husband had left. She didn't know where he had gone but he had made several trips recently to Miami.

'It's a saying we learn at police academy that flight is indicative of guilt. We put out a general alert for D'Arcy centring on Florida and told the Irish police that he had gone.'

D'Arcy had chosen the very moment to flee when the law was reaching out for him. 'Maybe he felt I was getting too close. Maybe he heard from one of his friends the kind of questions we were asking around.

'I don't think he sensed it from me directly because at no time did I ever accuse him.

'I was just asking him questions. But of course how much can you camouflage? Perhaps he could tell from the questions where I was driving.'

Five days later, on Sunday, October 15th, Imundi was on duty in his office when a call was put through to him from Miami police. A man calling himself John J. Quinn of Roanoke, Virginia, had been found dead in a bedroom of the McAllister Hotel. Two notes had been found by the bedside, both signed Patrick J. D'Arcy. Was this the D'Arcy New York police wanted to find?

Imundi flew to Miami to attend the police autopsy. He was shown the body still wearing the bottom half of a pair of pyjamas. It was certainly D'Arcy, even in death still wearing that roguish expression that the detective had come to know so well.

The Florida detectives told him that D'Arcy had booked into the hotel four days before on October 11th—the day after he had taken flight from New York. The hotel manager had become worried when the room had remained locked for three days and had called the police. A 'do not disturb' notice had been hung on the door.

The autopsy showed that D'Arcy had died from a massive dose of barbiturates. They had almost certainly come from an empty bottle of tablets found by the bed. A bottle of bourbon, drained almost dry, and the dregs of a drink in a glass were on the bedside table. And with them were a bunch of farewell notes in D'Arcy's distinctive handwriting.

Imundi read through the notes, wondering if D'Arcy had decided to clear his mind at the end by a confession. But right to the last, D'Arcy was giving nothing away.

Two of the letters were incongruously formal, the final acts of a man tidying up after himself. One gave the address of a Roman Catholic priest in Manhattan, the other asking for burial in a national cemetery.

Only in the third letter—addressed to his wife—did D'Arcy make any reference of a personal nature. He asked his wife for her forgiveness, but as Imundi observed: 'Forgiveness for what?

It was a privileged communication between husband and wife and we shall never know just what lay behind it.'

The coroner's verdict was that Patrick D'Arcy had committed suicide. He was buried at Dade Memorial Park on the outskirts of Miami.

From the Irish police the case closed with D'Arcy's death. Though no proof exists, they are satisfied that he killed Pinky Domenech on top of the Cliffs of Moher.

A motive is now of only academic interest. But it seems obvious that Pinky's death was precipitated by some kind of lover's quarrel. Perhaps she refused to go away with D'Arcy; perhaps he refused to give up his wife for her and lost control of himself when Pinky threatened to expose their affair to his family.

The New York police, for their part, have not yet been able to dispose of the case. Virginia Domenech is still officially missing — and will be for another four years until she either turns up or can then be legally presumed dead.

Why she disappeared is even more open to speculation. There is a strong probability it was connected with Pinky's death — the dates are too close together for coincidence to explain the mystery. D'Arcy was known to be back in New York the day she suddenly left her apartment. But how, or for what reason? The only people who can answer that now are dead — or have disappeared without trace.

GUY DENIS: FRANCE

The Peugeot Kidnapping

The Peugeot Kidnapping

Guy Denis is a pocket-sized policeman. Scarcely five feet tall, this sharp-eyed 'Napoleon of Detectives' was France's premier crime investigator in its toughest area, Marseilles.

Denis calls Marseilles the 'Chicago of Europe'. The region he overlords borders the blue waters of the Mediterranean and extends to Provence, the Côte d'Azur and the bandit-infested island of Corsica which he flies to visit six times a year.

Drug trafficking—prostitution, extortion, murder, fraud, revenge gang killings: these are the problems which confront Denis at the Hôtel de Police. The narcotics situation is so serious that the American Federal Bureau of Narcotics keeps a permanent office in the city. From his room in the grizzled, stark police headquarters building Denis can see out into the harbour and the sea beyond. Within a few hundred yards of his front door lies Château d'If, immortalised by Dumas in *The Count of Monte Cristo*, now a naval museum.

Denis speaks eloquently with eyes, arms and hands as only a Frenchman can. 'Today we started an inquiry into a financial swindle which will amount to many millions of old francs.

'Yesterday it was an armed robbery on a jewellers at Aix-en-Provence. That is Marseilles for you. This area is really the highest point in crime-fighting that you can find. For the policeman it's also very difficult, very hard on the nerves—tough physically and psychologically. There are times when one longs for peace and quiet, when one even thinks of re-signing in favour of a younger man.'

But Denis is a young fifty, in mind and in body. His greatest years are probably ahead of him: he has now become deputy director of the Police Judicaire in Paris. For France has not yet forgotten his achievement in solving a crime which scandalised the whole nation a decade ago.

In April, 1960, Eric Peugeot, four-year-old grandson of the millionaire head of the French car company, was kidnapped from the St. Cloud golf course on the outskirts of Paris. A ransom of fifty million old French francs (about £35,000) was paid over, the child returned safely to his family—and the abductors disappeared.

Eleven months later, in March, 1961, with the country and the government demanding results, Denis confronted the kidnappers at a French winter sports resort and obtained complete confessions.

All France was shocked by the crime. The nation applauded the man who had solved it so completely. Denis was awarded the Legion d'Honneur and his success gave him the entrée to French society and the friendship of some of the greatest families in the land. To them today he is still 'our detective'.

To achieve such fame Denis had travelled a long way from the days of his provincial upbringing—the son of a schoolteacher and town mayor in Lower Normandy, a boy whose early ambitions were directed towards medicine.

Denis comes from the little town of Flers. His father taught in the neighbouring borough of Argentan, home of Henry II during England's occupation in the Hundred Years War.

Young Guy Denis was in his first year as a medical student when war broke out in 1939. He joined the air force and, when the country collapsed a year later, enrolled in the police—a reserved occupation—to avoid being transported by the Germans to a forced labour camp.

'I went in merely as a way of getting through a difficult period. In normal circumstances I would have been a doctor now. But when the war ended it was no longer possible to go back to medicine. Besides I had become fascinated by the job.'

For the first year he was an inspector in the intelligence department at Poitiers, then joined the police college at St. Cyr and after the liberation was sent to Paris. In 1949 he was appointed the first head of the Paris region G.R.B. (counter-banditry squad) to deal with the frightening rise in organised gangsterism.

It was not until November, 1960, seven months after the kidnapping of Eric Peugeot, at a time when the trail was cold and the police were under fire for their lack of success, that Denis was asked to take over the case. The detective who had been heading the inquiry was transferred to another department and Denis given the clear-cut brief by the French government: 'Find the kidnappers; take as much time as you need — but find them!'

.   .   .

The Peugeot name is synonymous with the growth of France as an industrial nation as well as with the birth of the motor car. The history of the family goes back to the late middle ages: in the 1880s they established one of the first vehicle-making factories and by 1889 had produced a three-wheeler — the forerunner of the modern car.

The emphasis on a family-dominated concern however tended to hold back the Peugeot empire when its rivals had grasped the message of the consumer era — that to be rich one had to merge, re-capitalise and grow larger.

Today Peugeot has a business association with the nationalised Renault company and has had to sacrifice some of its individuality. But the name still stands for quality and reliability in an industry that is now committed to the mass-produced article. Ironically it was the position of the Peugeot name in the car-making world — neither too big and anonymous nor too little and unable to meet the ransom demand — that marked down the fair-haired Eric as the kidnappers' choice.

The French treat Easter as do most other civilised societies — a thanksgiving for the end of the dark winter days and a foretaste of the summer that is to come.

On April 12th, 1960, Paris was getting ready for the Jour de Pâques — Easter Day holiday. In his office in the Rue de Berri, M. Roland Peugeot, heir to the family fortune, then a board director, received an unexpected telephone call from a member of his house staff, Jeanne Germanio, nursemaid to Eric and his seven-year-old brother Jean Philippe.

Mlle. Germanio was in a flustered, excitable state and it took some time before M. Peugeot could grasp what she was saying: Eric had been kidnapped and a letter had been left behind marked: 'M. Peugeot, Most Urgent.'

That afternoon Mlle. Germanio and the Peugeot family chauffeur had travelled with Mme. Colette Peugeot and her two sons from the house at 170 Avenue Victor Hugo in the 16th Paris district to the St. Cloud golf course.

This was part of the routine of life for the Peugeots when they were in Paris. Husband and wife were both members of the golf club whose exclusiveness made it a centre of the social life of the great families of the capital.

While Mme. Peugeot played golf or gossiped with her friends in the club house, the two boys were turned loose in the private playground attached to the club where they could dig in the sand, slide down the playchute or generally frolic around among the trees.

It was the job of the nursemaid to keep an eye on Eric and Jean Philippe to see that they did not get into any trouble. But for an instant her attention was distracted.

One moment Eric was there, playing by the chute: the next, when Mlle. Germanio looked, he had gone. One of the children's playing companions, Carole Grawitz, told the nursemaid that Eric had been taken away by a man who had disappeared through a breach in the fence surrounding the playground. Jean Philippe Peugeot had heard the kidnappers say 'come along' and saw his brother go without a struggle. He said the man 'looked nice' and was about twenty years old. The gap in the fence had been made by tearing aside part of a flimsy wire mesh, itself hidden by an overgrown hedge.

The gap led to some deserted gardens. On the other side of the gardens was a gate, and through the gate a narrow cul-de-sac leading towards the main road. The chain in the gate had been cut and now it swung backwards and forwards on its rusting hinges.

Such was the security of the St. Cloud golf club. It was closely guarded at the main entrance to keep out 'undesirables'. Yet the back way had been breached in the most elementary manner.

An envelope lay in the sand at the bottom of the chute. In printed red block-capitals were the words: M. Peugeot, Most Urgent. The envelope was carried into the club house and handed to Eric's mother. She opened and read it. Then it was handled by any number of other people — destroying all hopes the police might have had of finding the kidnapper's finger-print on it.

The letter read: 'Dear M. Peugeot. This is what you will be able to read in the newspapers if ever you make a fool of us . . .

' "The Peugeot child, aged six [the kidnappers had the boy's age wrong: Eric was born in 1955; his brother was seven] is dead after having suffered horrible tortures because his dear parents have refused to part with fifty million francs [500.000 NF] ransom money, or because they have talked too much to the police."

'I don't want to put your child in the care of Dede. Dede is a good chap but he is a bit daft . . .

'However, if you want to see your child again, follow our orders exactly. When you have him back talk about it to the police if you want to, *but not before* . . .

'Get hold of the fifty million in notes of 10,000 and 5,000 denominations only. All the notes must be used. *We will not take new ones.* If you try to note down the numbers or mark the notes you will lose your child. (He will be given back to you after you have given over the money and we will carry out our side of the operation very quickly.)

'We will give you forty-eight hours to get this amount. Place the money in a briefcase which is locked (*keep the key on you*) and wait for new instructions. We will ring up your home in the next forty-eight hours . . . and don't forget that the life of your child depends on just the way you behave . . . .!

'Be reasonable, M. Peugeot. We believe in caution, and follow our instructions to the letter . . . ! ! ! !'

From his office, Roland Peugeot—in Denis' words 'trembling with emotion and overcome by the terrible threats hanging over his son'—rang the police, an action which was to precipitate a crisis within the Peugoet family circle in the course of the next few hours.

That evening the Peugeots, a strong, proud, close-knit family, held a 'conference of war' to decide what action should be taken to get Eric back alive and well. Finally it was agreed that the police should be kept out of the affair as far as possible and that the family should do exactly what the kidnappers wanted.

This decision in turn upset the detectives from the première brigade—Paris's equivalent of the flying squad—who had already been alerted by Roland Peugeot's first telephone call.

The police—with justification—did not like the way the case was proceeding. But they were on difficult ground. They were not dealing with ordinary people but with one of 'les grandes families', a household name whose ties with the highest ranks of government and civil service made tact and diplomacy essential.

'The family was absolutely distraught, in complete despair for two days. On that first, dramatic night, an argument broke out between the Peogeot family and the police.

'The Peugeot family wanted to carry out faithfully the instructions of the kidnappers.

'The detectives wanted to get started straightaway while the trail was hot. On the one hand, the police could already see the problems involved in tracking down the men. On the other hand, as human beings, they could understand the motives prompting the family to want to keep the police out.'

The story of the kidnapping had already reached the French newspapers and that same night, as the Peugeots and the detectives rowed over the next move, Eric's disappearance had already become world-wide news.

According to one version of the kidnapping, evidence had leaked out that one member of the Peugeot family was in collusion with the criminals to obtain money from Eric's grandfather, Jean Pierre Peugeot, sixty-four-year-old head of the business. At a much later stage, the family, with help from Denis, were able to clear its name of this terrible accusation.

But for the moment it did not help the strained relationships between the Peugeots and the police. As Denis comments: 'For a time there was an unpleasant feeling that the family was not revealing all the facts it knew.'

In the end it needed the intervention of the Minister of the Interior, Pierre Chatenet, to sort out the trouble which was threatening to cause a 'scandal within a scandal'.

'He decided that the police should do things in order. First we should give the Peugeots the chance to get back the child without having to worry about the work of the police inquiry.'

The Minister instructed the head of the Sûreté, Jean Verdier, and his opposite number at the Police Judiciaire, Michel Hacq, to go and see Roland Peugeot. They were to tell him that the police would not intervene in any way as long as the child was missing. The Peugeots were being given carte blanche to negotiate Eric's return.

All that the police did do — with Roland Peugeot's agreement — was to station a detective in the apartment in the Avenue Victor Hugo to keep details of all telephone calls coming in from the kidnappers.

The first genuine call was made that night from a man re-affirming the ransom demand. The next morning he phoned again. But it was never possible to trace the calls because of the automatic dialling system. Besides these there were many others from cranks, well-wishers and confidence tricksters offering bogus information in return for money.

On the morning of the second day of Eric's disappearance, the kidnappers sent a second and final letter to the boy's father. This one read:

'M. Peugeot,

'Meet you at exactly 1600 hours today, Thursday, in front of No. 57 Avenue des Ternes with the money. Hold your briefcase in front of you in both hands so that the messenger can recognise you.

'He will tell you "Keep the key". Only then must you give

him the briefcase. (But keep the key.) Under no circumstances give the key to him because this person does not know what it is all about. If the police arrest him, you will not be any further forward.

'I hope for your sake that nothing happens to him. If the police watch you it is not too late—if you really think you are being followed—to put off this meeting. Think of Eric above everything else. Do not make one single error as this will go against him. We will then fix another meeting.

'I repeat that we have set up a division between us and the messenger and anyone who is arrested by the police will not be able to help towards recapture of your child for the simple reason that he does not know anything.

'On the other hand, if it goes off all right, you will never hear any more from us: that will be the end. We have no intention of spending the rest of our days in prison. For another thing, Eric is nice and intelligent (very) and sweet but he is beginning to get bored and we are too.

'Even if you have not told the police, even if they are not familiar with the details of this letter, pay attention—we have ensured that your movements are constantly watched. Don't use your car—only the Metro or taxis.

'If you follow our instructions and advice you will get a call tonight telling you where you can collect your son. Keep your promises and we will keep ours.

'Above all, don't say anything to the messenger: simply give him the briefcase when he says the password "Keep the key."

'This operation must be carried out very quickly. If you talk to him he will certainly not accept the errand and all will be messed up.

'Warning: As I told you on the telephone last night only the orders written on this kind of paper and with this typing will be valid.

'This letter is the last one. Be sure that you are sensible about handing over the ransom. Throw off the policemen who might follow you and we will give you your child. If you don't pay

enough attention at the meeting place, if you are followed by
the police, if our messenger allows himself to be followed and the
next man in the chain is caught—then all will be lost. The
child is our surety and will not be returned if the ransom
doesn't arrive safely.

'We regret but we cannot do otherwise because of our own
safety: that is to say that if everything goes well at 1600 this
afternoon we shall give your son back late in the evening.

'P.S. To come to the meeting place, wear a hat and wear
sunglasses. That is very important.'

At the time indicated, Roland Peugeot went to the rendez-
vous fixed by the kidnappers. The handover of the money took
place in the Etoile district in the middle of the afternoon,
outside a passageway which led to the Hôtel Doisy. A man
came behind M. Peugeot, took the case out of his hands and
then melted away into the crowded street.

That night Colette Peugeot received a telephone call. The
speaker did not bother to stay long enough to identify himself.
He said: 'Go out into the street and you will find your son.'

At that very moment Eric was being confronted by a man
who had found him standing in the street, outside a lighted
café in the Avenue Raymond Poincaire only a few moments
from his home. Eric was taken inside and identified from a
newspaper photograph. He was cold but unharmed.

The switch had been made. Now, after cooling their heels for
forty-eight hours, the frustrated police could start work.

.   .   .

Denis uses phrases when retelling the Peugeot case like 'a
masterly affair' and 'the finest crime I have ever investigated'.
For him detection is a creative task: he thinks deeply about the
character of the criminal with whom he is in conflict, even
when the adversary as yet has no more substance than a
fingerprint or a sketchy eye-witness description.

He does not romanticise crime but sees in the pursuit of a
clever criminal an intellectual challenge. One of the questions

which puzzled Denis and his colleagues during Eric's absence and still concerned them morally after the boy's return was the degree of personal danger to which the child had been exposed.

Had the kidnappers intended to kill the boy as so often happened in such cases if they had failed to get the money? Might they have planned to kill him even if the ransom was paid out?

'This was a very delicate and disturbing question. One is justified in thinking they might have killed in view of the fact that we found a 9 mm. Luger pistol in their possession after their arrest.'

(This discovery, incidentally, was to be the watershed in the affair for Denis — its presence in the case enabled him to break down mentally the mastermind behind the plot.)

'In all fairness I must add that the kidnappers stressed their non-violent intentions, saying they only wanted to make some money and that on no account would they have killed the child. It is difficult to sound such depths of the human soul but I don't really think they had any deliberate intention of murdering him.

'One can however but wonder what might have happened if they had been caught in possession of Eric. They had hidden in a small house in the Ile de France right in the country. It is certain that if they had killed the child they could easily have buried him there in the middle of the countryside without any real risk of the body ever being found.

'It was a reasonable fear on our part but we cannot honestly say there was any proof of homicidal intentions.'

The police were disconcerted by the way the kidnappers had been able to do their work virtually unnoticed. The exchange of the money, the abandonment of the kidnap victim — these are the two points at which any kidnapper is most vulnerable. But in this case they had exposed themselves without being spotted either time.

Jean Pierre Peugeot, the president of the car company, had taken it upon himself to raise the money for the return of his grandson. But in doing so he personally did not feel obliged to honour the conditions laid down in the kidnappers' letter: 'If you try to note down the numbers. . . you will lose your child.'

With the aid of trusted members of the staff, the grandfather put the Peugeot accounts department to the job of recording the bank note serial numbers. The ransom money had been made up according to the instructions, in 5,000 and 10,000 franc notes. The numbers of £5,000 in old francs were recorded but there was not time to complete the job. In the end Jean Pierre Peugeot's sagacity, by a cruel irony, only served to hinder the police and to prevent him from ever recovering the bulk of his money.

While Roland Peugeot had gone on radio to plead to the kidnappers: 'My only concern is to get my child back safe and sound: I formally undertake to ask that the kidnapper should not be prosecuted', his father was drawing up the list of the notes for handing over to the police.

The police decided to publicise the numbers. By Easter Monday, four days after the return of Eric, the newspapers were running the list. This only helped the criminals. They were able to salt away the 'hot' money and were still left with £30,000 which was untraceable and could be freely spent. Apart from the odd note, none of the recorded money was found until after their arrest.

'Apart from this, the positive facts in the dossier were few: the crime was so out of the blue and the gang had been so lucky.'

An elderly gardener, working at a house adjoining the club grounds, said he had seen a man and a child get into a black Peugeot 403 and drive off. He said the man was thin and wore a green pullover and grey flannel trousers. The child did not seem to object to being taken away.

The butler of Prince Sadruddin Kahn, whose house led on to the cul-de-sac, saw a fair-haired man wearing a jacket and navy blue trousers at the wheel of a black Peugeot. He saw him back the car into the entry and wait with the engine running. But he did not see the kidnapper or the child enter the car. Another witness said the car driver had been small, stocky and was wearing a black beret.

By carefully questioning Eric's playmates, the police learned that the boy, who was by nature a quiet lad, had gone quite willingly with the kidnapper. The breach in the fence and the cutting of the chain on the gate had obviously been done well in advance of the crime itself. The black Peugeot had been seen parked in the cul-de-sac on days prior to the kidnapping and for a number of nights dogs in neighbouring houses had been disturbed by prowlers.

Among eye-witness accounts collected by door-to-door inquiries in the area of the golf club two, completely contradictory, stood out.

A cook at a house bordering the golf course on the Garches Road said that at about five o'clock on April 12th, she had seen a black Peugeot 403 pass by with two men in the front and a woman in the back. She was holding in her arms a child, aged about four or five, who was struggling.

Against this there was the story of a couple who, at the same time, had seen a car coming from the direction of the club on the main route into Paris. This car, again a Peugeot, black and type 403, had been halted at traffic lights. There were two men inside, one at the wheel, the other in the back seat who seemed to be concealing a live body under some sort of a cover. When the lights changed the car had sped towards Paris.

Eric Peugeot, when he was fit to be asked about his 'adventure', had told his mother that he had been taken by two men and that there was no woman in the gang. One of them had had the job of guarding him while the other was frequently absent. Eric told how he had been looked after in a large room furnished with a roomy divan. He had slept on this divan and his watcher had stretched out beside him at night. There was also a big farm-house table on which they ate. There was a television set and a telephone which sometimes rang but which nobody ever answered.

In one corner was an alcove for a wash-basin and beneath the bowl was a flush toilet. A firearm hung on one wall. Eric said the men, anxious to keep him happy, had let him mess about with the knobs on the television set and gave him playing cards to cut up. They had also fed him liberally with yoghourt.

The building was periodically shaken by a noise from outside which to Eric sounded like a passing train.

All this data led the detectives to prefer the evidence of the couple who had seen the Peugeot at the traffic lights to that of the cook. They considered that while Eric was held pending payment of the ransom he had been hidden in the residential quarter around the Bois de Boulogne.

A systematic house-to-house search was carried out over a two kilometre radius around the Arc de Triomphe. It concentrated on those houses beside the Metro and the above-ground railway lines in case the noises Eric heard had come from there.

Other policemen were following up the ransom notes and the telephone calls. The first letter, left in the sand in the playground, carried the trace of a fingerprint on the red typing ink. But the police scientists found only seven identifiable characteristics on the print, not enough to compare it with any in the criminal records files. What had made things more difficult for the forensic scientists was that the letter had been handled by several people when it was opened at the golf club. Some had never been identified and so it was impossible to eliminate their prints.

The envelope bearing the words 'M. Peugeot, Most Urgent' did not reveal any clues either. Its crumpled condition suggested that it could have been in the pocket of one of the kidnappers for some time. It led the detectives to suppose—rightly as it turned out—that the men had either tried to commit the crime on a previous occasion or had carried out a 'dummy' attempt.

Other detectives were concentrating on the identification of all black Peugeot 403s stolen or hired out within the preceding weeks. A further group were checking all possible contacts with the Peugeot family—their relations, servants, disgruntled ex-employees at the car factories, the members of the St. Cloud golf club, the caddies and everybody connected with the place. The chauffeur and the nursemaid were closely questioned but their statements did not reveal any contradictions.

It was an immense amount of effort—and it produced nothing constructive. The first sign of movement in the inquiry came at the end of April, 1960, when Paris police were told of the discovery of a burnt out black Peugeot 403. It had been abandoned in the countryside near Joigny, in the Yonne, about 100 miles south of the capital.

The wreck was that of a car, no. 1-CF 20489, stolen from the Etoile quarter of Paris on March 10th, a month before the kidnapping. It seemed that the tyres had been pulled off the car and thrown into the Yonne river which ran nearby before the vehicle had been set on fire. This implied the blaze was deliberate. Why? The detectives could only presume that the owner wanted to destroy all traces of his connection with the car.

If it was the car used in the kidnapping, the tyres might have been torn off to prevent comparison with tyre track impressions taken from the cul-de-sac behind the golf course.

One feature of the wreck puzzled the police. Minute examination revealed a slit in the metal bodywork surrounding the boot of the car. It was only many months later that they learnt the explanation for that.

.   .   .

The only direct evidence still to be followed up was the paper used for the ransom notes and the characteristics of the typewriter used to type them.

The paper came from the paperworks of Laroche Joubert in the Charente and bore the watermark of a dove in flight and the words 'Champs Elysées'. This particular batch of paper had been produced at the Basseau factory—but that was as far as the trail led. This kind of paper was supplied to multiple stores throughout France—the Prisunic, Uniprix and Monoprix shops where you can buy anything from a needle to a fur coat. It was impossible to track down where one single writing-pad had been sold.

The detectives then moved on to a study of the typewriting of

Germany's ace murder detective, Mathias Eynck. Patience and stealth are his weapons.

Werner Boost, marksman, hunter . . . and mass murderer.

Boost (fourth from left) and his accomplice (extreme left) at a masked identity parade. The men without masks are detectives.

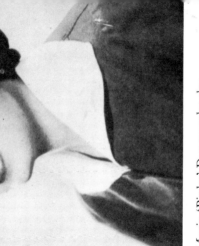

Maria 'Pinky' Domenech: she disappeared in New York . . . her body was found 3,000 miles away in Ireland.

The Cliffs of Moher in Galway: Pinky Domenech's body was cast over by her lover.

Detective Romolo Imundi outside a bomb-shattered Harlem police station.

Guy Denis, on the Marseilles waterfront. He tracked down the kidnappers of Eric Peugeot after other policemen had given up.

Four-year-old Eric Peugeot, heir to the French car family fortune.

Raymond Rolland and his beauty-queen girl friend, Lise Bodin.

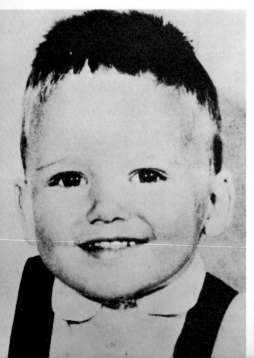

The cottage at Epiais Rhus outside Paris where Eric Peugeot was held until the ransom had been paid.

The room in the kidnappers' cottage described to the police by Eric Peugeot after his release.

The passage Doisy in Paris where the ransom money was handed over.

The Dutch detectives Toorenaar (right) and Jagerman at the telephone kiosk on the Rembrandtsplein in Amsterdam where they caught one of the gold-smugglers.

Roderic Knowles, London 'man-about-town' and mastermind of the smugglers' plot.

One of the gold-smugglers' 'corsets' seized by the Dutch police.

Richard Chitty, Scotland Yard detective who caught the police killers, returns to the scene in West London of the triple murders.

Harry Roberts, now serving thirty years in jail for his part in the murder of the three policemen.

the letters. The use of the red capital letters had probably been intended to dramatise the situation in M. Peugeot's eyes. But as capitals are less regularly used on a typewriter, there was the chance of finding some peculiarities which might help to identify the machine.

The letters were sent to the forensic science laboratory in Lyons. There, M. Gayet, the director of the laboratory, came up with some interesting facts.

The documents showed that the writer had had no formal typing training. There were many typing errors and they showed a complete ignorance of the rules of letter composition.

Besides this, M. Gayet noticed a bad alignment of the margin. A deeper study showed a number of points suggesting the type of machine which had been used:

The word spacing of 2.5 mm. suggested a French or Swiss made machine. German, American and Italian machines used a 2.6 mm. spacing.

The type face was 'Elite' with a 'Pica' spacing, made by the Setag company of Switzerland.

The space between each line was 4.10 mm.

Since all the lettering had been in capitals, a number of the letters showed up peculiarities—particularly the S, G, M, P, E and N.

Finally, the 'degrees' sign had a unique underlining which might at some stage clinch the machine's identification.

The police had already instituted their own search for the typewriter that had written the two notes. When this information from Lyons reached Professor Ceccaldi, head of the Paris police laboratory, he told his men to concentrate their inquiries among two typewriter agencies supplying machines with Setag type faces—the Houses of Japy and Hermes.

Both Houses seconded their chief technicians to help with the investigation. Although the 'Elite-Pica' type face was quite rare and the machine probably an old one, it still meant a colossal search. The production of this type of machine, made up of a number of models, ran into many hundreds of thousands.

After weeks of laboratory tests, the experts plumped for a

Japy office model, type S-17, made around 1952. The decision was not unanimous—some of the technicians disagreed with the choice—but a general call went out to everybody who had brought, hired or repaired such a typewriter.

The police investigation had now almost run out of steam. Occasionally one of the 'hot' bank notes turned up in Paris but it could never be traced back to its owner.

Then there were the hundreds of telephone calls and letters, many of them anonymous, offering assistance, putting forward crank theories or just attempting to exploit the Peugeot family's misery.

The detectives turned up the file on one of the extortionists who had contacted Roland Peugeot when Eric was still absent. From what Eric, on his return, had told his mother, the man appeared to have some special private knowledge of the crime.

Alain Peugeot, Roland's younger brother, had gone to a meeting-place named by the man. This man, having made some hostile comments about 'grandes families', had assured Alain that the boy was well. He said Eric was eating yoghourt and playing cards—both facts later confirmed by the child. But Alain Peugeot had quickly cut short the interview because the man had not been able to prove he was one of the kidnappers.

Several months later, Alain Peugeot had picked out the man among the criminal records files. He was tracked down by the police and confronted. His name was Penaud. He said his actions had been prompted by 'anti-social' feelings and begged forgiveness.

Penaud was allowed to go when it became clear that he could not have been in on the crime. And there was no evidence that he had really meant to extort money. But it was never satisfactorily explained how he came to know some details of Eric's confinement.

By the late summer of 1960 the investigation had slowed right down. The number of detectives directly involved had shrunk to a fraction of the original numbers: the impetus had been lost.

The police and governement were the butt of criticism for the lack of results. 'The kidnapping was a weight on the conscience of the community.'

At the end of October a top-level conference was held at Versailles between Michel Hacq, head of the Police Judiciaire and the public prosecutor. The decision was taken to inject new life into the case. The detective in charge was transferred to the Fraud Squad and Guy Denis was told to devote himself exclusively to catching the Peugeot kidnappers. From November 15th, 1960, the diminutive detective virtually turned his back on family life with his wife and three young children in their Neuilly flat for the most arduous task of his career: a fifteen hour, seven days a week job.

.   .   .

After the liberation of France, Guy Denis had the chance of entering the Civil Service. 'If I had done, I might by now have had a higher rank. But this job I am in is a very enviable one. It is above all tremendously fascinating. I have spent twenty-seven years fighting crime. My life has been dedicated to the pursuit of criminals. In Paris, Marseilles and Algiers there were many tense moments: in Limoges and Rheims, where I also worked, it was much quieter but still a challenge.

'The overall experience has been such a rich one on the criminal level. It has allowed me a much greater understanding of men.'

The job has also given Denis the opportunity of contact at all levels of society. In Paris these days, when time permits, he retains his interest in horses and his social contacts at the exclusive Club de Gentleman Riders. In his youth, Denis was a competitive jockey. His height, the broad shoulders, the sensitive hands and the watchful eye give him a professional's instinct for a horse. He gets up early to get in two hours' riding each day when the demands of the job allow it. 'More than anything else it helps to keep me in trim.'

None of his children have followed their father into the job —

few policemen's families do. It's a difficult career to combine with a family life. One of Denis's daughters is a doctor, his son is a chemist and his younger daughter is a barrister— Denis himself holds a law degree.

At first, as Denis relived the Peugeot affair in his gloomy, overcrowded office on the second floor of the Hôtel de Police, he remained impassive, sitting at his desk carefully explaining the work of those early months of the inquiry.

But when it reached the point where Denis took over the investigation, the memories of the happenings ten years before brought him excitedly to his feet. He punctuated the story with karate-like chops of the hands to emphasise points.

'When I was asked to take charge we were all very anxious and very afraid that we might fail. For us police it was vital that we should succeed. Kidnapping was, and still is, a pretty rare crime in France. To have failed would have been to run the risk of seeing this sort of crime on the increase. The implications were immense: the future security of families and children was at stake.'

Before starting his investigations, Denis and a colleague spent a fortnight re-reading every report on the case. The paperwork gathered over the previous seven months had filled a four foot high cupboard. It contained the anonymous letters, interrogation reports, scientific data and even all the press clippings. From these papers Denis set up a card index system of car numbers, suspects, witnesses and 'hot' ransom money findings.

Next the detectives drew up a list of ten possible trails by which the kidnappers could have escaped with their fortune. Each trail had a name: the first was the 'Bordeaux route' but this quickly petered out.

The second, which initially seemed very promising, was code-named the 'New York route.' Denis and his colleagues spent the whole of January, 1961, running this trail down. This tangent of the investigation demonstrated what policemen so often find in a major investigation—stirring the depths of the criminal underworld will bring other previously unknown crimes to the surface.

'What we eventually found in New York was a French gangster white-slavery operation. Their business was trading in women, finding girls in France and exporting them to America as prostitutes.'

What had alerted Denis was a tip that a known French criminal was leaving the country for America in circumstances which suggested he might be carrying the ransom money in his luggage.

'We had been told that a girl with whom he had been seen was flying to New York from Paris. The man was travelling by boat and they were rendezvousing in America. He had taken certain precautions to cover up his departure which made us suspect him as the Peugeot kidnapper.'

Denis had already booked his passage to America and the numbers of the ransom notes had been circulated there where Denis found that instead of a kidnapping he had fallen upon the track of a prostitution racket. The matter was then handed over to the Federal Bureau of Investigation. 'I cancelled my trip to New York because it was no longer worth it. I would have liked to go but this was no time for a tourist jaunt.'

A month before, in December, Jean Pierre Peugeot had made a personal approach to Denis asking him to conduct a private investigation into the case. But Denis declined, saying that it was not the time and he was not in a position to carry out an unofficial inquiry.

On January 20th, 1961, as the 'New York route' was already beginning to lead them along the wrong track, Denis and his team started the 'Interpol trail' so called because the international police organisation—headquartered in Paris—had tipped off the Police Judiciaire about the free-spending activities of two Bretons named Pierre Larcher and Raymond Rolland.

The original tip had come from an ex-policeman who had known Rolland for a long time and Larcher slightly. He had been surprised to see Rolland spending so freely in the April when he had been so hard up only a few weeks before. The identity of the informer has never been revealed by the police because he had asked for anonymity out of fear for his life. But the Paris evening paper *France Soir* published an article by the informant in March 1961 and said that it had paid him £750, the reward it had been offering for information leading to the kidnappers' arrest.

This information had first reached the police two months before, at the end of November, 1960. But at first there was nothing to distinguish it from the daily in-pouring of indecisive information.

Rolland, twenty-four, had a record as a small-time smuggler, the result of illicit trading in juke boxes. But otherwise he was unknown to the police. Larcher, thirty-two years old, was an entirely different personality. He was already on the run from the police—and had been since six months before the kidnapping. He had a lengthy record of violence, procuring, theft and fraud.

The police were told that Rolland had brought a ticket to fly to Rio de Janeiro but had later cashed it in at the airline office and had had his money refunded. He was known to be living on the Boulevard Suchet in the 16th Paris district with a Danish girlfriend, Ingelise Bodin. Lise Bodin, as she was better known, was a beautiful nineteen-year-old model who had just won the Miss Denmark beauty queen competition. She spoke English but hardly a word of French.

A check on Rolland's living habits showed that he had been living in style since about April 15th—three days after the 'snatch.' Since then he had been seen driving around in a series of big American cars, a Chevrolet Impala, a Studebaker and a Ford Thunderbird.

With Larcher 'not available' Denis first decided to investigate Rolland's background. He found that the man was divorced and that he and his former wife came from a respectable provincial background in the Sarthe.

The ex-Mrs. Rolland was finally traced to a small perfume shop in the Opera quarter of Paris. At first she refused to talk about Rolland: 'although he had left her, she still felt some affection for the man.' But eventually she told the police she had lent her own typewriter to Rolland on April 3rd, 1960. At that time Rolland was certainly no man of substance, having borrowed nearly £200 from his wife.

She said that she had tried to get back the typewriter from Rolland a number of times. He had finally explained its absence by saying he had lent it to a friend who had mislaid it. He then gave her another machine of the same make, but a much later model with a German type face.

The ex-wife was able to find letters and notes she had typed with the original machine. Comparison tests showed that the typing was similar to those on the ransom note.

She also told the police that she had bought the typewriter from a multiple store in Le Mans in 1951. A check with the shopkeeper revealed that it was a Japy with an Elite-Pica type face—but that it was type S-2000.

It was not the first time in the case—and it was not the last time—that the police had been led astray by well-intentioned but incorrect information. The typewriter experts, though not in complete agreement, had concluded that the ransom letters had been typed by a much later Japy, type S-17. The police descriptions of the typewriter circulated throughout the land had been based on this opinion. But as Denis said later: 'It was certainly a mistake. Still, we did know the essential characteristics of the machine.'

The detectives patiently probed deeper into Rolland's recent activities. They discovered that he had recently bought a Peugeot 404 in Paris. They got hold of the sales document and found that it showed the number of a bank account opened under the name of Rolland de Beaufort. Inquiries at the bank showed that in February, 1961, £1,785 had been placed in the account via a cheque from the Megève branch of the Annecy Commercial Bank.

The police at Annecy were asked to investigate this find. They discovered that Rolland and Lise Bodin were now living in a chalet at Megève called the 'Six Children'. It was the the height of the winter sports season at this Alpine holiday resort. Rolland and Bodin were living quite openly, keeping 'open house' to their many friends.

The Annecy police reported that there was at least one other couple and perhaps two living at the chalet. There were two cars parked outside, the Ford Thunderbird and the Peugeot 404, both of which belonged to Rolland.

Denis selected a six-man team to travel down to Annecy with him. French journalists had got wind that the case was nearing its climax and were following Denis everywhere he went. But the detectives managed to escape unseen from Paris, travelling by train, sleeping on board and then transferring to private cars. With them went Rolland's ex-wife who had agreed to confront him over the loss of the typewriter if Denis considered it necessary.

Denis and his team arrived at Megève on Saturday morning, March 4th. The local police, who were keeping the chalet under surveillance, told him that at least five people were inside.

Denis himself sensed that the end of the job was near: 'I was absolutely sure that these were the kidnappers. It was very important for me to have this deep inner conviction.'

He spent the Saturday with his team bringing their plan up to scratch. 'The secret of success in a case of this magnitude is to form an intimate team under one chief and use each man's talent to its best advantage.'

The chalet was pointed out to Denis across the snow-filled slopes. He and his team remained at a distance so that the inhabitants of the 'Six Children' would not take fright. Then the Paris detectives retired to Annecy for the night and held a final briefing session: 'It was essential for every man to know what was going on.'

The local police had told Denis that the occupants of the chalet breakfasted at about eight o'clock each morning. Denis instructed his men — more had by now arrived by road — to be ready to launch the raid between five and seven a.m.

But despite these precautions, Denis was upset to learn that Larcher and a woman and another couple had been able to slip through the cordon in Rolland's Peugeot 404 at six o'clock that morning.

'We were sure that nothing we had done could have prompted

Larcher's sudden departure. But you can imagine how worried we were. And we were no happier when we saw in a Lyons morning paper the headline "The Last Moments of the Affair" with underneath a story about the Peugeot kidnapping.'

Denis ordered road-blocks to be set up on all main routes. Then the police team entered the 'Six Children' chalet. They found only Rolland and Lise Bodin inside. Rolland said that Larcher was headed for Paris and was travelling through Switzerland, via Geneva.

Finally, at eleven o'clock the same morning, the police at St. Trivier de Courtes, about 100 miles away in the Ain, phoned through to say they had intercepted the Peugeot. Five hours later Larcher and the other three occupants arrived back at Annecy police headquarters under heavy guard.

Here, for Denis and the kidnappers, the most crucial hours of the affair were to be played out.

.   .   .

Megève had suddenly become the focal point of the case. Besides Denis and his team and the kidnap suspects there was a third group of people with more than a passing interest in the progress of the inquiries. Across the valley from the chalet of the 'Six Children' Roland and Colette Peugeot and their sons Eric and Jean-Philippe were winter holidaying in Megève at the very time of the arrest — a complete coincidence according to M. Peugeot and one in which the police had had no part.

The questioning of Rolland and Lise Bodin had already begun when the police arrived back at Annecy with the rest of the group. There was Larcher and his girlfriend Rolande Niemezyk, a twenty-four-year-old medical student Jean Rothmann, and a Japanese girl. Denis immediately decided to isolate the newcomers so that Rolland would not know they had been caught.

The interrogation of Rolland took up the whole of that day, March 5th. He was the one whom Denis was certain would crack first. 'What few facts we had were directed at Rolland.

Larcher I knew was a thorough professional, used to dealing with the police. I couldn't hope to get a confession from him yet.

'I had to get the admission first from Rolland who was not so experienced in police methods. The facts we had weren't enough—victory had to come the hard way: by an admission. If we didn't get that it was certain justice would not be done.'

In a three hour morning session, Rolland admitted nothing. But in the afternoon's interrogation he admitted that for a number of months up to the end of March, 1960 he had been living by his wits. He said the sudden change in his standard of living had come from the proceeds of smuggling.

Then the police carefully introduced the evidence of the typewriter—the only hard fact they had on Rolland apart from his sudden wealth. Without much trouble he admitted borrowing the typewriter from his former wife. But he said it had been stolen from his car on the Champs Elysées a few days later. Why, the police asked, had he not reported the theft? Rolland shrugged his shoulders. What was the use? The police were so inefficient.

As the interrogators pursued the question of the missing machine, Rolland became confused—a fatal mistake because it gave the other side a chink in his mental make-up at which to probe. By the end of this interview, Rolland was so mixed up that he was telling the police the typewriter thief might be his own friend Larcher.

The third and final interview took place at ten o'clock that night. 'Rolland got involved in a whole series of contradictions. Finally, at one o'clock in the morning, he confessed.' The vital admission was to a member of the Paris team, Leboule, whom Denis describes thus: 'A very able man, very courageous and with a good grasp of psychology.' In fact a man modelled on the lines of 'Le Patron' himself.

'Rolland admitted his part in the crime but played down his importance. He said Larcher—who at this stage he thought was still on the run—had played the major role. He said he had been terrified of Larcher and had been at his mercy. He said he had agreed—the knife against his throat, figuratively speaking

—to go and take the ransom money from the hands of M. Peugeot. For this job he had received £8,000.'

Denis, when the details of the confession were relayed to him, was inclined to believe that Rolland had played the minor part. Unquestionably he would have been under the domination of the other man. But Rolland's part in the crime must have been greater than he admitted if only two people were involved.

While this had been going on, Rothmann and the three girls were also being questioned. Rothmann admitted that he had allowed Rolland and Larcher to use his name for various business transactions. Larcher, posing as Rothmann's uncle and his father, had leased an apartment in the Rue Raffet and a room in the Rue Château-Landon in Paris.

Paris police were asked to follow up these leads immediately. In the Rue Raffet apartment they found some calculations on bits of paper which suggested the ransom had been shared out equally. The police also found there the Luger pistol wrapped in a Paris newspaper published about the date of the kidnapping. They also came across two apparently genuine passports, ready stamped, with pictures of Rolland and Larcher—but no names.

From the room in the Château-Landon, the police recovered typed notes made on a new Setag machine and an identity card issued to Rolland but in the name of Raymond Poleand.

Rothmann's Japanese girlfriend knew nothing about the kidnapping and she was later allowed to go free. Lise Bodin and Rolande Niemezyk could add nothing to the story but were kept in police custody for the time being.

With the evidence of the Paris finds, Denis decided to go back to Rolland, reveal now that Larcher had been under lock and key all the time, and ask him to confront Larcher with his allegations. It seemed the only way to penetrate the 'smoke screen' of silence Larcher had put up.

'When I told him that Larcher had been arrested he was very upset. It was only with some difficulty that we persuaded him to repeat his story in front of his companion.

'I had to arrange their confrontation back to back. Larcher

had such a strong personality, such a piercing stare, that he would have upset his accomplice. Then Rolland would have gone back on his confession and I would have been almost back at square one.'

Denis was taking a calculated gamble: he might 'win' or 'lose' both men by staging this confrontation. The two men stood there, facing opposite corners of the interview room, uniformed policemen warily watching to put down any signs of violence.

'Rolland was terribly embarrassed at having to reveal himself as the man who had "split". At one moment he was on the point of retracting his confession but finally he poured it out timidly and quietly.

'As for Larcher, he remained aloof and detached as though what was going on behind his back was nothing to do with him. But contrasting with his impressive calm, Larcher's looks betrayed a deep disgust for the other man. Rolland, having weakened, already seemed to be his enemy.'

Denis brought to an end this 'dangerous dialogue' as soon as he could. Time was against the police now—under the French 'forty-eight hours' law they had to tell the examining magistrate whether they had enough evidence to make out a charge. After those two days the police could not carry out any more questioning.

Alone in the tiny interviewing room Denis then faced Larcher, who he was now certain was the kingpin of the kidnap operation. It was to be one of the most moving experiences of his career. For the whole of the day Larcher held out—the plausible criminal pitting his mind against the tiny, voluble master detective in that drab C.I.D. office.

．　　　．　　　．

L'affaire Peugeot still retains its magic for Guy Denis. Out of respect for the family he changed cars from a Citroën to a Peugeot after the case. Today he drives a 404 cabriolet with the distinctive number 1 DG 13. He is regarded as a close and honoured friend of Roland and Colette Peugeot—Jean Pierre

Peugeot is now dead and Roland, his eldest son, has succeeded him as head of the business — and Denis proudly wears the ribbon of the Legion d'Honneur in his buttonhole.

But such fame was not easily won. It was already a very tired Guy Denis who began the battle of wits at Annecy police station against Pierre Larcher by enumerating all the evidence (largely Rolland's testimony) against him.

'Larcher sat opposite me, saying nothing because he knew that if he talked he was lost. I kept the conversation going for three hours without getting more than twenty words out of him. The really crucial stage lasted from ten that night until three o'clock the next morning. The tension was extraordinary: time was running out. I was more worn out than he was.

'Then came the moment when he suddenly cracked — without any warning. I find there is often this moment of psychological shock in a criminal that triggers off a confession.'

Denis had one ace left up his sleeve — the discovery of the gun in Larcher's flat. He decided to use it to try to provoke the man across the table. He told Larcher of the finding of the weapon. 'I suddenly leant forward and told him: "You vile animal. To all intents and purposes you are a murderer. If M. Peugeot hadn't given you the money you would have killed that child".'

The sudden accusation seemed to unleash the confession Larcher had been keeping in check. 'Larcher said, "M. Denis, believe what you like but I can't let you believe for a moment that I would kill a child." All the time Larcher had been most correct and formal in his speech, never using the "tutoyer" (familiar) form which we often adopt in interrogations.

'As Larcher said these words he threw himself at me with his hands at my throat as if to say "Not another word."

'Larcher felt he was lost. He was furious at being caught out and yet — to his credit — wanted to put the crime in its right perspective: a kidnapper, yes; a child murderer, no.'

As he described the scene, Denis stood at one side of his desk, both hands round his throat, jerking his head backwards in a graphic reconstruction of the events in the interview room at

Annecy. 'I can still remember it as if it was only yesterday.

'I pushed him away. The door was partly ajar and I had colleagues outside who could have protected me. But Larcher was a bit theatrical like that. This kind of questioning always has an air of drama about it.

'He stepped back and I said to him: "If you really want me to believe that you are not a murderer tell me exactly what you did. For the moment, since we found that gun in your flat, I am forced to believe you intended to use it on the child."

'Perhaps to defend himself against this accusation he agreed to confess. Then he was overtaken by a sort of nervous breakdown. He sobbed, he put his head on my shoulder and wept like a child. My attitude softened at that. I said: "Listen old man, you can relieve your conscience." He thought he was going to get prison for life but I told him the most he could get was twenty years' penal servitude [the sentence which he and Rolland eventually received]. This gave me the moral ascendancy. From that moment on he was completely candid.'

By then it was four o'clock in the morning and this last session had been going on for six hours. By eleven that morning the forty-eight hours would be up. 'I was by now at the end of my tether.'

Denis had almost lost his voice; he could hardly see to write — he had had no sleep for four days and nights — but the confession had to be recorded within the next seven hours and preferably as soon as possible, before Larcher had time to think again.

A colleague came in and took down Larcher's story while Denis, tired but triumphant, crawled off to bed.

Larcher told how difficult life had been for him on the run from the police since September, 1959. While hiding out in the country he had decided to go through with the crime. Larcher said he had been obsessed since adolescence by the story of the Lindbergh kidnapping — he was thirteen when it happened — and had read every account he could lay his hands on.

'The desire to realise it came to him when he read the French translation of a novel called *Kidnap* by an American writer, Lionel White. I have read this book carefully myself

and found in it a man, the leader of a kidnap gang, upon whom
Larcher very much modelled himself.

'In it the gang leader is in Paris with no money. He gets the
idea of carrying out a kidnapping. He needs for this a family
rich enough to provide fifty million francs in twenty-four hours.
He needs a child aged three, four or five at the most: not too
young because of the risk of it dying and not too old because
then the child would remember everything and might struggle
to defend himself.' The first ransom note was copied almost
word for word from *Kidnap*.

To choose the perfect victim, Rolland had bought a copy of
the Bottin Mondain (the French *Who's Who*) using a false name
and address, Philippe de Scala, living at Villa Ursula, Paris 11.

The police later found this book and the receipt for its
purchase in Larcher's apartment in the Rue Raffet. On page
1341 under the page headed PEU the entry against 'Peugeot,
Roland' had been boxed in with a pen. It gave the family's town
and country addresses and telephone numbers and the details
of their children with the year of birth: 'Jean Philippe (53),
Eric (55).'

The idea of snatching one of the Peugeot children had
replaced in Larcher's mind an earlier scheme involving the de
Rothschild family. It seems that they did not have any descen-
dants of the right age.

'Afterwards we had a tip-off about another projected kidnapping, certainly organised by the same gang. They were
aiming this time at another important family—in the furniture
business—who had a very considerable fortune: enough to
pay a £100,000 ransom. In view of their earlier success, they
were putting up the price.'

At the beginning of January, 1960, Larcher and Rolland had
taken up position near to the passage Doisy, the place chosen
for receiving the ransom. Larcher lived near there in a small
furnished flat and Rolland in a hotel under the name of
Polland.

On March 1st, Rolland rented a small house at Epiais-
Rhus, a tiny village near to Grisy-les-Platres. It was a place

known to Larcher because he had been hiding out there for some months.

On March 9th, Rolland stole documents relating to a Peugeot 403 he had hired. That night both men stole a similar black car and altered its licence number to fit the documents they had stolen.

The Peugeot family had been away from Paris on a winter ski-ing holiday at this time. They returned to the Avenue Victor Hugo on March 16th.

On that date, Rolland began to keep daily watch on the movements of the family. He hid himself in the boot of the car, parked close to the Peugeot home, and observed their comings and goings through the narrow slit in the bodywork—the gap which had so puzzled the police when they found the burnt-out vehicle.

Soon Rolland knew that each afternoon Mme. Peugeot, the two boys and the nursemaid would be driven by the chauffeur to the golf course at St. Cloud.

'Here was the ideal victim and the ideal opportunity. In just a few days they had accumulated enough information for the perfect kidnapping. It was as simple as that—and very astute.'

The next move was to spy out the golf club. To do this Larcher dressed in a dark suit and a chauffeur's peaked cap while Rolland played the part of the 'young master', sitting in the back of the car to reconnoitre the scene.

The dogs barking around the club on the night of April 9th suggest that that was the date when the two men cut the chain on the gate and made the hole in the fence leading to the children's playground.

Two attempts were made to carry out the kidnapping before the plan succeeded. The two men had stolen a Peugeot because they reckoned that Eric would be more willing to get into one of his father's cars. They were right: he went with them unhesitatingly.

With the benefit of hindsight, Denis could see now where the police had gone wrong in their early investigations. Far from heading back to Paris, the kidnappers and Eric had driven out into the country to the hide-out at Grisy-les-Platres. So much for the evidence of the cook who had seen a car with a child struggling in the arms of a woman. And so much for the testimony of the couple who had seen the car with a boy inside heading towards Paris.

Basing their deductions on this evidence, the police had gone in entirely the wrong direction. 'Once again human testimony —as opposed to unshakeable scientific proof—had shown its disconcerting fragility.'

The sound of engines which sometimes rocked the kidnap house had come from the neighbouring aerodrome of Cormeilles where Air France pilots were being trained. And all the time the police were searching alongside the railway lines in the heart of Paris.

The descriptions of the kidnappers given to the police again showed up many discrepancies. Rolland said he had been wearing a grey pullover and not a green one that day, while Larcher was not wearing a black beret but an ordinary hat.

At the kidnap house Rolland had looked after the child and kept him occupied while Larcher had gone out to dictate the orders to M. Peugeot. For safety's sake he had gone each time to Paris and had telephoned from public call-boxes at busy Metro stations such as the Opera.

After abandoning Eric on the Avenue Raymond Poincaré outside the café, the kidnappers had abandoned the car in a Paris street. On their return to Grisy-les-Platres they had burnt Eric's hat and tie which had got left behind and also the briefcase which had held the money.

The final act in the plan had been to return to Paris to reclaim the Peugeot and then drive it out into the country and set fire to it to get rid of any possible identifying marks.

On April 22nd, nine days after the kidnapping, the house at Grisy-les-Platres was cleaned from top to bottom and then deserted by the two men.

Their activities in the house over the seven weeks they had lived there had not escaped the notice of neighbours. In the tiny village of Epiais-Rhus, any stranger was quickly noticed. Yet nobody ever thought to tell the police.

The day they left the house, Larcher checked into the Hôtel Lutetia in Paris under the name of Pierre Lauren. He told Rolland to act cautiously at first, not to splash his money around. But Rolland, described by his companion as the 'impatient lover', flew immediately by Caravelle to Copenhagen to meet up with Lise Bodin and begin his life of luxury.

.   .   .

Larcher's recital had taken nearly five hours to record in the Annecy police station. There was just enough time left within the forty-eight hour rule to arrange one more confrontation between the two men. 'This time when Rolland heard the facts revealed by Larcher—a man whom he considered his better and did not even dare "tutoyer"—he readily admitted his real role in the affair.'

That night the police convoy drove back to Paris, Denis and his men fatigued but knowing they had won, Larcher and his satellites realising they had lost heavily.

On the way there were two more pieces of drama. First one of the policemen had a heart attack brought on by exhaustion and had to be left in hospital at Dijon. Then, when they reached the outskirts of Paris, Larcher directed them to a garage he had rented in a false name in the 16th district. Inside was a parked Fiat 500.

Larcher told them to look inside the boot. There, in a plastic bag under the spare wheel, the police found £4,285— the notes whose numbers had been recorded by Jean Pierre Peugeot.

Rolland later told the examining magistrate that he had thrown the typewriter, borrowed from his ex-wife to write the ransom notes, off the d'Iena bridge into the Seine. But although police frogmen and divers searched the river around this point the typewriter was never recovered.

France exulted in the captures. The director general of the

Sûreté gave a luncheon in honour of Denis and his colleagues. That night Denis went on to the French service programme of Radio Luxembourg to discuss the case. Asked by the interviewer if the police could not do their work without such 'distasteful' methods as the use of informers, Denis said this certainly was not true of the Peugeot case.

'Under a democratic system there must always be informers. Without them the police could not operate efficiently.' (The truth of this statement was underlined some years later when detectives working under Denis in Marseilles recovered £200,000 worth of paintings stolen from the Geneva home of M. Martin Bodmer, vice-president of the International Red Cross. After a tip-off from an underworld informant, the Marseilles police found the paintings hidden under the hotel bed of one of the thieves—before they had even been reported missing by the Swiss authorities!)

Roland Peugeot went to the Sûreté Nationale to express his personal thanks to the police, and Jean Pierre Peugeot sent a letter of congratulations to the Minister of the Interior with a cheque for £3,600 for the police orphanage fund.

From March 7th, 1961, the night Denis saw Larcher and Rolland under lock and key in the cells at Versailles, until the day of the trial, October 27th, 1962, he never spoke to the two men again. From the moment of their return, the case was in the hands of the examining magistrate.

But Denis's job was far from finished. He now had to carry out mandatory commissions—checking points of detail in the evidence being accumulated for the Assize trial. This led Denis and his team throughout Europe in the footsteps of Rolland and Lise Bodin.

'From the month of June, 1960, Larcher and Rolland, accompanied by their girlfriends, had largely gone their own ways. Rolland was living a sparkling life, moving from country to country, Larcher leading a more sober existence.'

Rolland and his girl were easily traceable by the big cars they travelled in, the expensive hotels they stayed at and the money they flashed around. On their return from Copenhagen, a week after the ransom had been paid, they had booked into the four-star Grand Hotel in Paris. Then they moved along the Riviera, into Spain and Portugal.

The Chevrolet Impala they had been seen in together turned out to have been stolen from Anvers in Belgium. In this car they had driven the length of Europe, from Denmark down to Madrid via the Côte d'Azur. All along the route, Rolland had been changing the ransom money into foreign currency.

The trail led the police to London where Lise, as Miss Denmark, had been taking part in a Miss World competition. 'She was accompanied to London by Rolland and they had spent a considerable amount of money there. It was part of our job to try to ascertain just where the Peugeot's cash had gone.'

When finally Denis had finished this part of the affair—his travels on the heels of the couple had taken him from Finland to Portugal, from Britain to Berlin—the Algerian political crisis was at its height. At the end of December, 1961, he was sent to take charge of the Algiers region police service. 'It was not a happy time. We were right in the middle of the war and we police had to confront two sorts of terrorism: one the Algerian rebellion, the other the O.A.S., the hopeless terrorism of Algerian-born Frenchmen.'

Denis returned from Algeria after independence in time for the trial of the Peugeot kidnappers. Their girlfriends and Rothmann, the young medical student, had been set free as there was no evidence they were connected with the crime.

At one stage Larcher and Rolland retracted their confessions which they had claimed had been obtained under police pressure. But the recovery of the ransom money had put the result of the case beyond doubt. On the opening day of the Assize hearing, in Denis's presence, both men once again made complete confessions. 'If Larcher had not told us where the money was hidden we would never have had the formal proof that he was the kidnapper.'

The two men had also alleged collusion in the kidnapping with a member of the Peugeot family and a third man. But in court they withdrew these accusations.

The case lasted four days but Eric was not asked to give evidence. Medical witnesses told the judge that he still showed some fear of his kidnappers. His dreams showed anxiety and his pride at being the hero of the affair might distort the truth of his evidence.

The jury were out for only thirty-five minutes: both men received the maximum sentence, twenty years. The court awarded the Peugeot family the symbolic one franc damages. It ordered restitution of what remained of the £35,000 ransom money—about £8,750: the cash found in the boot of the Fiat, £1,785 in a bank account, a farmhouse the men had bought and their four cars.

It was ironical that the kidnappers' taste for good living let them down in the end. Larcher had taken meticulous care not to make the mistakes which had trapped the gang in the *Kidnap* book—abducting the nurse with her charge and having a woman in the gang.

'But Larcher did not realise that it was impossible to turn the characters in a novel into real-life figures without taking some account of human nature. It was women—the men's free-spending to impress their girlfriends—which led largely to their downfall.'

Once the case had finished, on the advice of Denis, Roland and Colette Peugeot instituted proceedings for libel and were awarded damages against French and German newspapers which had suggested they were implicated in the kidnapping.

'It is absolutely certain that there was no collusion between the family and the kidnappers. This version of the story was put about by certain friends of the criminals. If there had been any collusion it would have been a hideous plot to get fifty million francs from the grandfather. It would have been a most dreadful thing—and it was quite false.'

The accusations had begun in the early stages of the case. 'We could do nothing until the case had been successfully completed. People's reaction to me would have been: "You are on their side but you don't seem able to solve the case."

'Once the case was over we were able to defend the honour

of the Peugeot family before the courts. But it was terrible that they should have had to bear this after going through the agony of the kidnapping itself.'

Did Denis ever feel any sympathy for the kidnappers? 'It may seem strange for anybody who isn't a policeman to understand my feelings. We wanted so much to succeed that when success came—through luck or ability—we felt not exactly sympathy (the crime was too horrible for that) but a certain compassion.'

GIJS TOORENAAR: HOLLAND

The Smugglers' Trail

The Smugglers' Trail

Diamonds are a smuggler's best friend. They are easily hidden: man's appetite to possess them is insatiable. They are one of the world's great trading 'currencies'.

But to Gijs Toorenaar, head of the Amsterdam C.I.D., they are the source of a never-ending stream of crimes. Holland, one of the centres of the diamond market, attracts more than its share of swindlers. They range from common thieves to counterfeiters and forged cheque 'droppers'.

Toorenaar is a specialist in fraud, a connoisseur of the ruses of the confidence trickster. He keeps in the drawer of his desk at police headquarters in Amsterdam's Elandsgracht a memento of the fraud which almost milked one of the world's largest corporations, the Bank of America, of $600,000.

The souvenir is a Christmas card, an English hand drawn print of Trafalgar Square, Nelson's Column and pigeons on the wing. Today, now that the characters in the case have dispersed to the ends of the earth, it is the only reminder of five hectic days in the summer of 1968 when, in one swoop, he broke up an international diamond and gold smuggling ring and thwarted the fraud on the bank.

The message inside the Christmas card is quite formal: 'To Superintendent Toorenaar with best wishes from Jane Coleman and Roderic Knowles.' At first glance the true purport of the card is quite beyond the outsider. But Knowles was the man Toorenaar put behind prison bars and Jane Coleman the girl whose wedding plans he upset. It isn't every day a policeman gets remembered in this way.

One of the popular images of fiction is the perpetual 'war'

that is waged between policeman and criminal: two irre-concilable sides of society. Where violence is a feature of the crime a residue of bitterness may remain with a policeman even after he has secured a conviction. But most feel an element of sympathy with the wrongdoer. The normal 'cops and robbers' relationship certainly did not apply to Toorenaar and Knowles, Old Etonian stepson of Lord Swinfen (family motto: Through difficulties to the heights).

Knowles was what Toorenaar terms 'a gentleman crook', a member of the 'swinging London set' before he ended up in an Amsterdam jail. Detective Sergeant Evert Jagerman, Toore-naar's colleague in the fraud department, says of Knowles: 'He was a very nice boy, honestly he was. We were very sorry for him. He had worked so hard at his game.' Toorenaar amplifies this. 'He and his colleagues weren't criminals, only adventurers. To us Knowles is a friend. We were even invited to his wed-ding.'

Amsterdam was only one stage in a trail of smuggling and fraud which stretched from London, through Europe to Hong Kong, then into Korea and finally into communist territory in the north. In Toorenaar's words: 'It all came to grief because of the dreadful thoroughness of the Dutch mentality.' Knowles had planned to get money from the Bank of America with which to bolster up a smuggling operation that was rapidly running out of funds.

But it was in the Dutch city that one of Knowles' assistants, Peter Connell, a young Australian actor turned gold courier, made the false move which enabled the Amsterdam detectives to trap the conspirators—and dissolve their dreams of unlimited riches.

By the end of his investigation, Toorenaar had collected the names of twenty men, most of them British. They ranged from the carriers—'pawns' as the Dutch police called them—up to Knowles and Ben Smith, the Far East 'head of operations'. Most of them were like Knowles, young, intelligent men who had turned to crime as a way of getting a 'kick' out of life and a means of paying for an extravagant standard of living.

The operation had begun early in 1968 from a first-floor flat in Courtfield Gardens, Earl's Court, centre of West London bedsitter land. The carriers (or 'couriers' in smuggling parlance) were recruited from the Situations Vacant columns in *The Times* newspaper. The advertisements were deliberately ambiguous in words but hinted vaguely at 'rewarding travel opportunities'.

There were about 100 replies to the advertisements. A room was hired at the Cumberland Hotel in London's West End and twenty-seven men were invited to attend preliminary interviews. Five failed to turn up: the remainder were shown before a 'selection panel' consisting of three men and two girls.

The applicants were first told that the jobs were in the 'import-export' business. But during the interviews, the real aim of the operation became clear: gold was the commodity. The significance of this was obvious. Export of gold was then banned from Britain and the interviewees were told that if they did not want to get involved in an illegal enterprise they were free to leave.

Those who were still interested were then shown a folder marked 'Procedure' which listed instructions for collecting air tickets, carrying the gold and making delivery.

All but five of the men who turned up at the Cumberland Hotel said they were willing to go through with the work. They were shown specially-made blue body corsets with pockets sewn in for carrying the gold. Asked why they still wanted to go, all said they wanted to travel and the idea of some excitement with £200 at the end of it all appealed to them.

Where the applicant's credentials satisfied the 'selection board' he was asked to come for a further interview at Court-field Gardens where Knowles had rented a flat. The inter-viewee was told to have a cholera vaccination first and to bring along his British passport—foreign nationals were of no use in the operation.

This is how one man, a university student, described his first job for the gold smugglers in an interview in *The Sunday Times*. 'Before I was sent off on my first trip, I was told that if I was caught the sentence would be three months behind bars. I've never done anything illegal before and I kept wondering whether I really needed the £200 so badly.

'I was telephoned one evening, after several days of anxious waiting. I was told to pick up an envelope at the Swissair counter at Heathrow Airport.

'As I drove to the air terminal, I can remember thinking to myself "It's too late to want to become a clerk in an office somewhere."

'My instructions were to go to the Hôtel Beau Rivage in Geneva where I would be contacted. Twenty-four hours later, a slightly built Frenchman presented himself. Then began the corset fitting. The Frenchman lifted the harness out of his case with the tenderness of a priest about to robe a novice.

'It was light blue, a sort of rough nylon, and I noticed immediately that the stitched pockets contained the thin sheets of gold. As I stripped and slipped into the harness I felt my knees buckle slightly. My contact, like a solicitous tailor, hovered around me, tightening the straps and padding my sides to make it fit the curve of my body. After walking up and down the room several times, I put on my clothes and examined myself in the mirror.

'Just to test my nerve, we went down to the bar. A glance from the lift operator seemed like a fixed stare at my waist. Every pair of eyes I met seemed to have X-ray vision. I kept thinking: "My clothes are a useless camouflage—they all know I am carrying gold." A couple of drinks later, I felt better.

'On returning to my room I was told I had an hour before my plane took off. Where to? I would know when I went to the airport. Another envelope.

'My instructions were to go to Hong Kong on a non-stop B.O.A.C. flight. Although I can't prove it, I suspect a more senior member of the gang was on the plane to keep an eye on me.

'Half an hour away from Hong Kong my mind became numb. The harness was beginning to feel uncomfortable after the 18-hour flight. The procedure booklet told me always to stay neat looking, so I went for a shave. I had to hold the razor tightly to stop my hand shaking.

'Customs was a nightmare. There was a long queue and after the immigration barrier, I strolled casually to my case and the Customs officer. It was an anti-climax. Nothing happened and I walked away without suspicion falling on me. But I kept thinking that a bar would drop out of my corset on to the floor.

'At the Hilton Hotel, I relaxed on the bed for a few minutes before there was a knock on the door. A Chinese, immaculately dressed, shook my hand and said: "A good trip?" I stripped and passed him the corset. He folded it carefully, placed it in a suitcase and left the room saying: "Hong Kong's a good place. Have fun."

'When I got back to London, I found that £200 had been deposited in my bank account. The lure was too much. I made another trip but it was to be my last. It is nerve-breaking work. After my last job on the Geneva run, I told them I was quitting.'

.   .   .

Knowles had constructed a brilliant plan: but he lacked the approach of the born criminal mind and knew too little of the problems of buying and selling gold illegally. On the black market, the business was most profitable in those countries which operated high taxes on its importation — India and other Asian countries. Hong Kong was a natural jumping off point because of its position on the commercial trading routes between the west and communist China. The nearer to China, the higher were the rewards: up to £500 for one half kilo gold bar.

Even so, for the syndicate of men backing the gold smugglers — apart from Knowles and Ben Smith there was the owner of a London gaming club — the business was rapidly becoming unprofitable. The operation stood or fell by the prices it could get for its gold in Hong Kong and neighbouring territories. With the activities of the police counter-smuggling squads in the colony and the severe penalties for those caught, several gold 'runs' failed even to cover the expenses of the game. Some of the syndicate were pressing for the return of their investment and Knowles was in danger of running foul of those who were backing him.

Then, in April, 1968, a chance meeting in the bar of the President Hotel in Hong Kong between Smith and an American business man offered the smugglers the chance to finance all their future activities on the strength of one crime. It also provided Knowles with the idea of trading in diamonds as gold had proved so difficult to market.

Edward James Smith, known to his friends as Ben, was a Londoner who had graduated to smuggling from film stuntman and croupier. His role in Hong Kong was to organise the receipt of the gold from the couriers, to make sure it got to the Chinese buyers and to handle the payment for the job. The American, whose identity was subsequently revealed to the police, must remain unnamed for reasons which are explained later in this story.

He was on holiday in the colony with his wife from his job in Seoul. They met Smith and over drinks Smith said he was interested in gambling. The talk led from the roulette tables to making money, then on to the subject of gold. Smith confided that he handled gold shipments and the American told him that if it was a question of smuggling, the biggest profits were to be made in Korea.

The American said he had a plan which could earn the right organisation $2,000,000. 'I have been walking around with it in my mind for six years. What I need is an organisation ready to put it into effect. What you need is financial backing. If you will give me fifty per cent of the stake I think we could do business.'

The American said that he could get hold of confidential documents belonging to the Bank of America from their head offices in Seoul. If Smith was willing to help, they could photostat these documents.

Smith said he would first have to contact his partners in

Europe. If they were interested they could come to Seoul and continue the negotiations.

Toorenaar learned about the Far East end of the operation several months later when he was questioning the smugglers they had picked up in Holland. 'Mr. Smith is a man with a very bad memory. He forgets everything. So he sends Knowles a telegram which says in effect: "There is a scheme here which will make us as much money as we want. But I cannot understand the details. Please come to Hong Kong, you know all about figures and accountancy."

'Smith was so stupid that when he arrived in Korea with Knowles he had lost the American's address and it took them two days to find the house.'

The trip was something of a busman's holiday for Knowles. To pay for the journey to Korea he took the Australian, Peter Connell, along with him. Both wore the smugglers' corsets, each with ten kilos of gold inside. Their experience in Seoul trying to sell the gold should have been a portent of the troubles ahead.

In Korea, the hazards facing the smuggler were greater even than in Hong Kong. With the communists willing to pay any amount to acquire gold, Korea was certainly one of the most lucrative markets in the world. But the U.S. Central Intelligence Agency, with its network of informers in the south, was on the lookout for any sign of smuggling to the north, regarding it as a sign of hostile — almost espionage — activity.

It was a very dangerous game: far more was at stake than Knowles ever realised from the security of London. It was not unknown for a suspected gold runner to end up in a back alley with his throat cut.

Knowles was assured by the American that he would make a one hundred per cent profit on the gold he brought in. But when he and Smith arrived in Seoul they found only one man, a Chinese, willing to take the bullion. And when eventually they made the sale, under the eyes of the Americans, they got paid with sackfuls of small denomination notes.

To export more than a certain amount of currency from South Korea was a serious offence. It was a nerve-racking business for Knowles to change the money into notes large enough to smuggle it back to Hong Kong.

Smith and Knowles spent a week as the guests of the American at his house in Seoul. Connell, who was low down the organisation's hierarchy and was not needed for the business discussions, stayed in Hong Kong and spent the week golfing and surf riding: 'The most wonderful time I have ever had,' he told the police later.

On the Sunday morning of their stay in Korea, when the bank was closed, Knowles, Smith and the American got into the offices and photographed the documents they would need in the fraud. The most important result of their espionage was the acquisition of the bank's secret code system. The code, which was changed daily, was the bank's method of testing the validity of telegrams relating to the transfer of money between branches. If the telegram contained the code—a three-figure number—this authorised immediate payment by a branch to the person named in the message.

The bank 'spies' also took copies of past telegrams so that they could use the right word formula for such transactions. Besides this they made photostats of Bank of America letter of credit documents and the list of all the bank's branch managers in the world. It was the American's intention to use these later for a further fraud on the bank: but for the moment they concentrated on the more straightforward telegrams fraud.

The American, always talking big money, wanted to go for the 'jackpot' prize of $2,000,000. But Smith and Knowles were afraid that greed would be their downfall. Smith's argument was that such a haul could not fail to attract other criminals: they would then be on the run from both the police and the underworld. Finally they decided to go for the more 'realistic' target of $600,000.

They agreed to put the plan into operation simultaneously in Zürich and Amsterdam on August 2nd and August 5th, 1968, two visits to each bank, yielding $150,000 on each occasion. The telegrams would go off from Hong Kong in the name of the Hang Seng Bank. The dates were chosen to give them the maximum amount of time to get the money away before the fraud was discovered. August 2nd was a Friday and August 5th coincided with a bank holiday in Hong Kong.

At the end of the business discussions in Seoul, Smith returned to Hong Kong and Knowles to Europe. First Smith, now calling himself John Stevenson, had to establish himself as a man of substance in the eyes of the Bank of America. But this needed money. The smugglers were so hard up that the American had to lend them $10,000. He transferred this to Smith's account in Hong Kong and over the next few weeks this money went round and round. Only a tiny proportion of it was spent: nearly all the sum was used to create a façade of wealth.

Smith would authorise payment of $6,000 through the Bank of America in Amsterdam to Connell, who was using the alias 'John Nicholas Robinson'. Connell had instructions to send the money back—less $500 for expenses—to Smith. He then wired it off to the Zürich branch of the bank because it was urgently needed there to establish the credibility of the Zürich operator, a man equipped with a false British passport in the name of 'John Brown'. When the money got to Zürich, back it would go again to Hong Kong and then on to Amsterdam once more.

Knowles had by this time moved his headquarters from London to Brussels where he installed himself in the Hilton Hotel. London had only ever been an organisational base for the smugglers. Because of the restrictions on gold exports, England had proved too uncomfortable for the gang. Instead, they bought their gold in Switzerland and diamonds in Holland, because in neither country was it an offence to export: no licences were necessary.

Knowles left behind in Courtfield Gardens a man to recruit more carriers and to act as the liaison between them and the agents in Europe. When Holland or Switzerland notified Knowles that gold or diamonds were ready for the smuggling route, he 'ordered' from London the exact number of couriers for the job to go to either country.

The plans had been meticulously laid. Connell, alias Robinson, in Amsterdam was to draw the money on the pretext of the false telegram, buy the diamonds and then rendezvous with Knowles who would bring the couriers with him. Brown in Zürich, after getting the money, would go to Geneva and hand it over to another agent, 'L'. 'L' would buy the gold, order the carriers through Knowles and they would collect it in Geneva.

But the plot fell apart in Amsterdam. Toorenaar gives two reasons for its collapse: 'The inhibitions of the Dutch about paying out large sums of money so close to a weekend; Connell's inability to play the part of the wealthy young diamond merchant.

'Connell may have been an actor but he was a pretty bad one. He was in Amsterdam for three weeks rehearsing for the great day. Every other day he would go to the bank to manipulate some of this money that was floating back and forth between Hong Kong and Europe.

'He told the bank he was a diamond merchant but he said too much. One of the staff asked if it wasn't dangerous to transport diamonds out of the country with so many thieves about. Connell said: "Well, I am in an organisation that knows ways of getting them out of the country."

'He left the impression "smuggler" in the mind of the bank official. And it all went wrong from that moment.'

.   .   .

Roderic Knowles had taken infinite pains to make sure the smugglers who worked for him at £200 a trip and the agents in the field were as immune from detection as possible. He drafted a set of working rules—which he called 'Procedures'— for both agents and carriers. Jagerman, who later found copies in Knowles' hotel room, called them 'The Smugglers' Bible: the Dos and Don'ts of the business'. Knowles had seen the operation in military terms. In his orders he referred to the bank frauds as 'D-Day in Amsterdam and Zürich'.

These were the instructions found by Jagerman which Knowles had drafted to cover every eventuality.

The first set was for the London office to cover the Brussels route. Those carriers who were going to Belgium to pick up their 'loads' always travelled by boat-train from Waterloo. They were issued with a bag with special lettering on it so that the London organiser could recognise them at the station. In these instructions 'C' stands for carrier; 'Load Number' is the job number; 'FE' stands for Far East.

DAY PRIOR TO DEPARTURE

1. Always telephone the station to check time of departure of the boat-train to Brussels on the following morning, even though you already know (just in case of unexpected cancellation or sudden change in time-table).

2. *IF THE TRAIN HAS BEEN CANCELLED.* Re-book 'C' on an earlier train (on the same route, if possible) OR on a later train, provided that it does not arrive in Brussels later than midnight of the same day. If 'C' is booked on a later train, notify man in Brussels immediately by telephone. . . or send telegram express rate as follows:

'23 late 2230.' (That is '23 [i.e. Load No.] late 2230' [i.e. 10.30 p.m., being time of arrival at Brussels station].)

3. If all trains have been cancelled on the original route, book on another route provided that train does not arrive in Brussels later than midnight of the same day.

4. *IN THE EVENT OF ALL TRAINS BEING CANCELLED ONLY.* Book 'C' on a flight to Brussels. BUY SINGLE TICKET TOURIST CLASS. Pay for ticket by cheque if necessary. Notify 'C' by telephone OR by telegram as follows:

'23 Flight 2230.' (Interpretation as above.) — Time of Arrival at terminal.

As well as giving 'C' his plane ticket, having escorted him to the airport, give him also his boat-train ticket with which he will return from the Continent to London.

5. If it is impossible for any reason to send off a 'C' on the

correct day, to arrive in Brussels not later than midnight on the correct day, notify man in Brussels by telegram as follows: '23 Cancelled from London.'

Man in Brussels will then know that he is to use and despatch one of three of the reserve 'C's permanently stationed in Brussels, and he will be able to change the name on the ticket in good time, and notify FE of change.

6. IF IT IS IMPOSSIBLE TO SEND OFF 'C' ON CORRECT DAY, DO NOT SEND HIM AT ALL. He must not be sent, instead, two days later, unless that 'C' happens at the last minute to be unavailable. The planned rotation of 'Cs' must not be disturbed. The cancelled 'C' may be fitted in on the next unbooked trip.

7. *ON THE DAY PRIOR TO DEPARTURE, TELEPHONE* '*C*' to confirm that he will be arriving at your office not later than 8 a.m. the following morning. Remind him that it will be rush hour, that there would be no harm in him arriving earlier but certainly no later. If 'C' is not based in London, it would be advisable if you could arrange accommodation for him for the night.

On the telephone, remind 'C' to have the following items with him the next day: Passport, Medical Card, Visa (if required). Any business material that he has been instructed to bring, one large light travelling case, one small overnight case with toilet requisites and plenty of reading material, light coat or macintosh or camera (to hold in his other hand) AND REMIND him that he must wear the correct suit (wide trouser legs, etc., which has been approved by us—OTHERWISE HE CANNOT BE DESPATCHED).

MORNING OF DEPARTURE

1. 'C' arrives at your office at 8 a.m.—not later. His train leaves. . . station at. . . One of you will escort 'C' to the station in a taxi. If you intend going by car, two of you must accompany 'C' in case of any difficulty in parking which might delay you.

2. *AT OFFICE.*

CHECK OF LUGGAGE AND DRESS: Get 'C' to put on suit which you have already set aside for him. SUPERVISE his dressing. CHECK that laces are tied loose enough for comfort around his legs. *SEE ALSO THAT HE IS WEARING CORSET.* (If 'C's own numbered suit has been left by him in Brussels, then obviously he will collect his suit and corset there.)

CHECK WITH 'C' THE FULL CONTENTS OF HIS POCKETS AND WALLET, as well as the contents of his luggage. His trouser pockets must always be empty and remind him that he is to keep them empty at all times during his flight and especially when he is embarking at final destination. *Any* address book, or notebook with telephone number or address *and* any diary *must be taken* from him and kept (in a sealed envelope, with his name on it) until his return.

CHECK OF DOCUMENTS. 'C' must have on his person: Passport, Medical Card stamped up to date (CHECK VERY CAREFULLY) and visa if required.

TO BE GIVEN TO 'C':

(i)   £10 in cash.

(ii)   His boat-train ticket.

(iii)   CARD WITH ADDRESS OF HOTEL IN BRUSSELS where he is to go and remain until contacted.

(iv)   Packet of DEXTRASOL*

(v)   Must have a belt (or braces).

(vi)   New shoe-laces.

(vii)   Needle and cotton, safety pin and buttons.*

MORNING OF DEPARTURE

AT OFFICE: Give 'C' copy of 'PROCEDURES' for 'Cs' to read before leaving. 'C' is never allowed to retain a copy or to take one away even temporarily for any reason.

From the moment 'C' arrives in the office ONWARDS he is not allowed to make a telephone call (particularly after he has been given his cash, ticket and contact instructions). *NO* 'special circumstances' are to be accepted.

ORDER TAXI IN GOOD TIME.

AT STATION. Suggest to 'C' that he buys plenty of additional

---

*The Dextrasol was a sugar compound to give the carrier strength. The needle and cotton were for emergency repairs if the corset started slipping.

reading material. Buy yourself a platform ticket and remain on platform until the train leaves. 'C' is not allowed to make telephone calls at the station. If he wants to rush off and spend a penny, suggest that he does so on the train.

REMIND 'C' that if he is asked at Passport Control where he is going (on leaving England), he is to say that he is going to Brussels for a few days. If he is asked where in Brussels, he can say that he doesn't know exactly as his girlfriend is meeting him in Brussels at the station and they will be going to her family's house.

There were also briefing instructions which agents in Europe were to give the carriers when they picked up their smuggling jackets before stepping onto a plane for the Far East. 'M' stands for manager or agent.

THE FOLLOWING INSTRUCTIONS WILL BE GIVEN BY M. IN EUR. TO 'C' RE. HIS CONTACT IN F.E.

Tell 'C' that a car will be waiting for him at the airport, which will take him to his hotel: that the driver will be waiting for him as soon as he is clear of the Customs hall at the airport with the carrier's own name displayed on a plaque either held in front of him or displayed on his lapel. 'C' must announce himself.

'C's' arrival at the airport will be watched. 'C' is not visibly to acknowledge recognition of anybody, should he in fact recognise anybody.

On arrival at hotel, 'C' will find that a room has been booked for him in his name for two nights. He is to go straight to his room and wait there.

In the event of failing to make contact with the driver (he may have been unavoidably held up) do not wait around at the airport, take a taxi to the President Hotel and wait in the entrance-hall lounge. If you are approached by the hotel staff, say that you are waiting for a friend and that you are not sure whether he has booked you into this hotel or not and that you are expecting him to arrive shortly.

There were also orders laid down for paying carriers.

PAYMENT OF 'Cs'.

Always pay 'Cs' in U.S. dollars.

'Cs' are to be paid £150 *only*. (£10 will have been given to them on their departure from London. £40 will be withheld from them and they will be paid this balance of £40 that is due to them on their return to Europe WHEN, AND ONLY IF, THEY HAVE RETURNED THEIR 'SUITS' AND COR-SET.

You must brief them to this effect.

When they return to Europe, they must leave their suits and corset in a parcel IN A LOCKER at the AIR TERMINAL in the city. They must then put the KEY and RECEIPT in an envelope, with their Christian name and initial of their surname enclosed, and send it to JOHN ST. JOHN* at the address of the hotel at which they previously spent the night before leaving for the Far East.

ON NO ACCOUNT MUST SUITS OR CORSETS BE RETURNED IN ENGLAND OR EVEN BROUGHT BACK INTO THE COUNTRY.

Knowles established very strict rules of business etiquette for dealing with the 'small fry' couriers.

RELATIONS WITH 'C' AND BRIEFINGS.

1. Remember that 'Cs' do not know their Far East destination and they will not do so until they have arrived at the airport in Europe.

2. Remember also that 'Cs' are not to know their destination in Europe until the morning of their departure when you present them with their ticket.

3. 'C' is not permitted to know the correct name of his contact either in the F.E. or EUR.

4. Contact in EUR will be known as John.

5. If any 'C' shows himself to be unreliable in any way or gives you personally any reason for doubting his ability to carry out his part of the job, then you have our authority not to

*JOHN ST. JOHN was the code name for the 'head of European operations'.

engage him or to postpone his trip until one of us has had the opportunity to talk with him.

6. You are to deal with 'Cs' authoritatively and punctiliously (in exact accordance with prescribed forms). 'Cs' confidence in us, which is one of the utmost importance for us as well as for his own confidence, can only be undermined if he should find reason to believe that every aspect of the entire operation is not run with the maximum of discretion and absoluteness of discipline.

7. No. 'C' is to be given information, or have access to information, other than that which directly concerns him in the performance of his own particular task.

Even the payment of salaries and expenses had to be governed by the 'Procedures.' 'R' stands for Knowles.

ALLOWABLE EXPENSES

1. *CARRIERS.* (i) A £10 cash advance to each 'C' on the morning of his departure to Europe.
This is a payment on account of his fee. You are not authorised to pay him anything in excess of this.

(ii) Return boat-train tickets for 'Cs', tourist class to Europe.

(iii) You are to re-imburse 'Cs' for passport photographs, BUT NOT for any other expenses in connection with their trip, unless you have written authorisation from one of us.

2. *MATERIALS FOR SUITS.*

3. *FEES FOR MAKING OF SUITS.*

4. *SALARIES* (to be paid *in cash*). See overleaf. Insurance stamps are to be paid by individuals themselves, as they wish. No tax deductions to be made.

5. *TELEPHONE, HEATING* and *RENT BILLS* (and *ELECTRICITY*).

6. *TELEGRAMS.*

7. *SUNDRIES.* Stationery and small office materials. NO capital items unless specifically requested and authorised. Postage: milk, sugar and coffee. Flowers.

8. *SOLICITORS BILLS. NOT TO BE PAID* until approved by 'R' and having his signature on the bill.

INSTRUCTIONS RE PAYMENT OF SALARIES.

1. Salaries always to be paid IN CASH. Everybody must sign a Petty Cash Voucher on receipt of their salary. No insurance stamps are to be paid for and no tax will be deducted.

Finally, Knowles imposed a strict veto on communications between members of the organisation.

COMMUNICATIONS

Never, NEVER, make telephone calls from *your* hotel to:

(i)   Airport.
(ii) Abroad.
(iii) Or to 'Cs.'

NEVER send telegrams from the hotel.

EMERGENCY PROCEDURES

IF IT IS IMPOSSIBLE TO SEND OFF 'C' ON THE CORRECT DAY, DO NOT SEND HIM AT ALL.

He must not be sent, instead, two days later unless that 'C' happens, at the last moment, to be unavailable.

The planned rotation of 'Cs' must not be disrupted.

The cancelled 'C' may be fitted in on the next indicated trip.

You will inform him of this and arrange for his return to London.

.   .   .

On Friday, August 2nd, Ben Smith in Hong Kong received a call from the American in Seoul. It was the check code for the Bank of America for that day: 813. Smith had two telegrams ready. He incorporated the code in both and sent them off to the branches of the bank in Zürich and Amsterdam.

Knowles had already placed his agents in both cities. He had driven over from Brussels with his fiancée, dropping off Connell in Amsterdam and 'John Brown' in Zürich. In the Swiss city the fraud worked perfectly. Brown collected $150,000 from the bank which paid out without hesitation. He immediately travelled to Geneva and gave the money to 'L', the gang's operator there.

The man in Geneva knew nothing of the fraud. His instructions were merely to set up the gold buying and await the day when money would arrive to purchase the bullion. It was Knowles' policy that the cells in the organisation should operate in ignorance of what was happening further on along the chain. In this way there was less chance of the operation failing if one man was caught.

'L' followed his instructions. He already had the necessary business contacts in Geneva set up to buy the gold.

Once he had bought it he sent a telegram to Knowles in Brussels saying: 'Switzerland has worked.' Knowles rang London and ordered three carriers to be sent straight to Geneva to rendezvous with 'L'.

But even before he had heard from Geneva, Knowles was on his way to Amsterdam to collect $100,000 worth of diamonds and the rest of the money in cash.

Things had gone badly wrong in Amsterdam however. Connell, posing as John Robinson, had called in the morning to collect his $150,000 which he had warned the bank a few days previously would be arriving 'from my partner in Hong Kong'. When he got there, Connell was told the money had arrived. He requested immediate payment.

The bank teller who sensed that all was not well with 'Mr. Robinson the big diamond merchant' has since been promoted by the bank authorities. Connell's manner of talking had left him doubting the man's genuineness. As he told Toorenaar later: 'Friday. . . $150,000. . . a lot of money to carry around over a weekend. . . Mr. Robinson. . . smuggling. . . he's only had an account with us for three weeks. . . big businessman. . . lives in a tiny rooming house. It all added up to a big smell.'

The bank teller told Connell that because of the size of the withdrawal further inquiries would have to be made. He asked if Connell would mind coming back on the Monday after head office, in San Francisco, had cleared the transaction. Connell tried to threaten and bluster but nothing would move the bank. He finally left, a shaken, angry man, intending to get out of Holland as soon as possible.

He met Knowles at a bar in Amsterdam that afternoon and told him of his failure to get the money. Knowles too was annoyed, but for a different reason. He was sure that nothing could go wrong with the plan. He told Connell he was stupid for having made a scene at the bank. 'You are going back to the bank now to apologise for your behaviour and you will tell them that you are coming in on Monday to collect the money.'

Connell returned to the bank. He said he was sorry for having lost his temper and with the assurance that the $150,000 would definitely be waiting for him on the Monday morning returned to his lodgings.

Knowles went back to Belgium that night to find news of the success of the Swiss coup awaiting him. He felt he had been right in telling Connell to wait in Holland until Monday. Zürich had been a success: there was no reason to believe that the Dutch bank would sense any fraud.

As he told Toorenaar later: 'I thought that I would be a millionaire in a couple of days: well, at least a very rich man.'

But Knowles did take one precaution. He cabled Smith in Hong Kong—contrary to all the rules of prudence he had himself laid down in the 'Procedures' documents—telling him not to send the second batch of telegrams that were ready for the following Monday. Knowles feared that if another demand for $150,000 arrived at the bank before the first had been cleared this would jeopardise the whole scheme.

Unknown to the conspirators, the trap was already closing round them. After Connell's second visit to the bank a telegram had gone off to the group of banks administering the affairs of the Hang Seng Bank in Hong Kong.

It read: 'Today we received the following tested cable from the Hang Seng bank, Hong Kong. "Reimburse yourselves Bank America San Francisco. Pay us dollars 150,000 a/c John Nicholas Robinson order John Stevenson Hang Seng Bank."

'Immediately after receipt of this cable Mr. Robinson called on us and required a substantial amount in cash.

'Mr. Robinson with British passport and staying in a small hotel in Amsterdam opened three weeks ago an account with us.

Please check with management Hang Seng Bank whether this payment order is correct and reply by return cable.'

At ten o'clock on the Saturday night the reply came back from Hong Kong: there was no record of a John Stevenson ever placing $150,000 to be paid out to John Robinson. The Bank of America manager in Amsterdam drove to the police head-quarters and placed the facts in front of the duty C.I.D. man. Toorenaar, who was at home entertaining Dutch friends recently returned from Canada, cut short his party and contacted Jagerman. Both went straight to their office.

The tale they heard from the bank manager was a variation on a theme that both had met many times during their years handling fraud work. The yearly influx of tourists inevitably brings in its wake a flood of forgeries, in money and in traveller's and bank cheques. The holidays are the peak of the 'cheque dropping' year: the upsurge of dud credit is so predictable that Toorenaar and Jagerman make it a rule never to take these days off.

Toorenaar is resigned to the situation. 'Every year we know we are going to get some international crook leaving his "calling card" all over the city. Take 1967 for example. On Christmas Eve we got a call about a Mexican. He had arrived a couple of days before and was going round getting diamonds from stores and dealers with a stolen cheque book. He was using ten aliases.'

Two years later it was a massive bank fraud that misfired all for the sake of a few pence. Letters of authorisation, purporting to come from banks, were sent to Amsterdam banks ordering them to pay money to the person named in the document. The letters were perfect forgeries: the banks would have paid upon demand without question—if they had received the letters.

'Many thousands of pounds were involved. Yet the crooks had failed to put the right amount of stamps on the letters. They were returned to the banks who were supposed to have sent them out. The banks opened them and found that no such transactions had ever been authorised.

'We kept a watch on the banks, waiting for the people to come in and collect their money. But they must have been told that it had all gone wrong and never showed up.'

In many ways that fraud was a copy of the Knowles affair. Both failed because of elementary mistakes. 'Most of them do. Where they don't make errors it is honestly very difficult to catch them. When you are playing against swindlers you are up against men of great ability and charm. I don't mind admitting, some of them are cleverer than we are.'

But Peter Connell was not in that category. When Toorenaar and Jagerman had heard the bank manager's story, they were still not certain that any crime had been committed. 'We thought the amount of money involved was unusually big. But the bank told us it was quite normal. They said that something like £4,000,000 comes to Amsterdam every week in deals from the Far East.

'The bank said that if these men had withdrawn $50,000 once a week they would have paid out. But they had got too greedy.'

In such a case where there was no certainty that a crime had been committed Toorenaar works on the principle that 'if it smells let's first take in the suspect. If it's all okay, let's shake hands, dust him down, apologise and tell him to enjoy himself in Amsterdam.'

It's not difficult to imagine the effect upon a suspect of the combined persuasive powers of Toorenaar and Jagerman: 'we are as close as that,' they say, crossing their fingers. Both fluent in three languages, they are the perfect foils for one another: Toorenaar's straightforward approach balanced by Jagerman's warm friendliness.

Toorenaar first checked the police hotel control system which records all foreigners staying in the city. Connell (under the name of Robinson) showed up staying in a large hotel. But when the police checked there he had moved to a small rooming house on the Rembrandtsplein — Amsterdam's night club centre. He was staying there with a woman whose name turned out to be on another list: the register of prostitutes. It seemed to tie in — three weeks in Amsterdam, leaving a hotel to live in with a prostitute.

'But we didn't want to go straight to the address,' Toorenaar explains. 'We frankly didn't expect to find him. We thought he would have fled the country after being spotted by the bank. Experience has taught us that if you go to an address and the man isn't there, once you tell the prostitute who you are after you will never find him again.'

The two policemen first toured Amsterdam's red light district trying to find out if Connell had been seen in the prostitute's company. Several bars knew her but had no idea, or would not tell, where she was living. Nor did they know who she was living with.

Jagerman telephoned the address of the house on the Rembrandtsplein. 'A lady's voice answered. She said: "Hello, hello." I didn't know what to say. Finally I said "I'm sorry but I must have the wrong number" and rang off. At least we knew there *was* a woman there but we weren't much further forward.

'We tried some more bars, but still no luck. Finally, at one o'clock on Sunday morning, we said "What the hell!" and decided to go openly to the house.'

The door was opened by a grey-haired lady of about sixty years. She had the same name as the prostitute — but there all similarity ended. The detectives showed her the picture of the prostitute and asked if it was her daughter. She said she had never seen the woman before. They did not tell her what had been in their minds.

Toorenaar asked if anybody was staying in the house. 'No, apart from one Englishman, a very nice boy named Robinson, but he is asleep now.' Toorenaar took the key to his room and the two detectives went in. They searched the room for ten minutes while 'Robinson' lay asleep in bed. Then they woke him up.

'Are you Mr. Robinson?'

'Yes, what do you want. What's going on?'

'We want to talk to you. It's about a prostitute.'

'I've never heard of the girl. And I've never been with a prostitute.'

At first he seemed frightened and on edge, but when Toorenaar mentioned 'prostitute' he relaxed and became indignant. The detectives had already found, and then replaced, a British visitor's passport in the name Robinson. Now they asked him to produce it and bring it with him to the police station.

They merely told him that thay wanted to check him out. 'He came quite willingly. We didn't tell him what we were really after. When we are dealing with swindlers we like them to tell the story.'

Toorenaar has a firm rule when dealing with 'con men'. He says: 'Never believe a swindler. If you tell him what you know he will immediately try to alter the facts. A swindler lives on his wits. He is trying to swindle us too. Ask him if a suit is black and he says: "Sir, yesterday it was green, perhaps tomorrow it will be black." He can never give a direct answer. It is only when you press him for a reply—"What is this?" "What, sir?" "This." "This?" "No, this."—that he will give you your answer. Otherwise never.'

First Toorenaar asked Connell to tell his story. 'We didn't contradict anything or try to trip him up. Then we gave him what we call "food for the brain".'

This consisted of planting seemingly innocuous questions in Connell's mind with just enough information to start him wondering what they really know.

'What are you doing in Amsterdam? What is your business? Have you ever heard of Mr. Stevenson? Have you ever been to Hong Kong?'

'Okay. Now he's got food for his brain. We leave him in the cell for several hours and he starts thinking "Well, what do they know?" '

The story Connell told at that first hour-long interview was that he was a diamond dealer with a partner in Hong Kong. 'That's an interesting profession,' Toorenaar remarked idly. 'How do you send your diamonds to Hong Kong?'

'I give them to another of my partners and he takes them across.'

The detectives asked for the name of this partner. 'Well, I don't know his name but I meet him at a pre-arranged rendez-vous in Amsterdam. I will know him because he is a typical Englishman, carrying an umbrella and wearing a bowler hat. I give the diamonds to him.'

By so mixing fact and fiction, Connell was telling what Toorenaar termed later as 'a ridiculous, extravagant James Bond tale'. Connell said the detectives could check his credentials with the Bank of America. 'I've just received $150,000 from Hong Kong, you can check on that.'

'Oh? Well, we'll ask the bank.' No mention was made by the detectives of the fact that they already knew this.

Jagerman brought the interrogation back to the story of the man with the bowler hat. 'Were you really going to give $150,000 worth of diamonds to someone waiting on a square; someone who carried an umbrella; someone whose name you didn't know?'

'Yes, that's how we often operate in the diamond business.'

Toorenaar put Connell in the cells to 'sweat it out' while he went back to the lodgings with Jagerman. They were looking for documents: 'Swindlers lie, but their papers don't. In this kind of case you must work almost wholly on documents. It is important to get hold of everything: even a bus ticket may help.'

In Connell's room the detectives found his real passport, an Australian one made out in the name of Peter Connell. They compared the two passports. The one issued to 'John Robinson' was a forgery and not a very good one at that. The imprint of the British Foreign Office stamp was missing from the photograph.

The Dutch police frequently find that forged British visitor's passports turn up in Holland. These are mainly used for day trips to the continent. They are valid for one year and cost only seven and sixpence. All the prospective traveller needs to produce at his local employment office is a birth certificate, two photographs — and the passport, in the form of a card, is made out while he waits.

'Our experience suggests that it is all too easy to get your hands on them. It seemed funny when we first found the passport that an important diamond merchant should be travelling on one of these.' Later Scotland Yard told the Amsterdam police that Connell had bought a copy of a birth certificate in the name of John Nicholas Robinson the day before the passport was issued in Willesden in North London.

Connell was brought back to the interviewing room. Toorenaar asked why he was carrying the visitor's passport. 'He told us a nice fairy tale but we said: "No, sir, that's not quite true. This is a false passport, isn't it? And you are not Mr. Robinson".'

Connell readily admitted his true identity when he saw the other passport in Toorenaar's hands. 'We could tell from the way he acted he wasn't a real criminal. I said, "Boy, you are in something that isn't really your line of business. It's too big for the likes of you".'

Connell had no strength left for the game of bluff. 'No, sir, that's true. I'm dying with nerves if you must know. For three weeks I've been so frightened I haven't been outside the house apart from going to the bank. I have just sat at home with Aunt Martha (his landlady). One day when I met one of the bank employees in the street I nearly died. I thought they were following me.'

Connell explained the whole operation to the detectives in a statement which was not finished when they broke for sleep at seven o'clock on the Sunday morning. The interrogation restarted that afternoon and in this session Connell told the policemen about the Zürich end of the operation. By the evening, when he had told everything, he was in tears.

Jagerman says of the young Australian: 'He is a very nice boy, indeed he is. I told him: "Boy, you are far away from home." You must have what we call "contact" with a suspect. You have got to find a subject that is close to his heart. Maybe it's his mother or his grandfather. With Connell it was motor-racing. I don't know anything about that but I told him about Zaandvoort, out Dutch grand prix circuit and it seemed to get through.

'You see, when I do this I am being both a detective and a human being. You can be with a swindler. But it's different when you're dealing with a killer, for instance. With him it's difficult to establish an understanding.'

Connell was pressed for details of the Zürich job. But he said he knew nothing apart from the fact that what he had done in Amsterdam was going to be repeated there.

Toorenaar phoned Zürich police and alerted the Bank of America officials in Holland. But it was not until Monday morning they discovered that the $150,000 had already been withdrawn on the basis of the false telegram. And by then Jagerman's studies of Connell's notebooks had uncovered an entry which was to lead straight to the gold smugglers.

Every time Connell did business at the bank he had to sign with his pseudonym 'John Nicholas Robinson'. He had kept copies of all his practice attempts at writing the name. He kept a bank statement which showed that he had sent money to a Mr. Smith in Hong Kong.

Then there were lists—page after page—of mathematical calculations. This was Connell working out the intricacies of carat weights. He knew nothing at all about diamonds. Before meeting the diamond merchants from whom he was to make the purchases Connell had brought reference books to read up the subject. The impression of the diamond dealers he met was that he was a complete innocent: 'Strange kind of diamond buyer he is, but if he pays why should I grumble,' said one.

Among the pages of calculations of carats, Jagerman found this entry: OOOXOPOLOOOO/50. 'I asked him what this was about. He gave me a story but I felt he was lying. So I started talking about his family—his father owns a tiny gold mine back in Australia. You cannot ask a question directly of a criminal. If it is important, you must move round and round it.'

In the end the answer came out: the entry was a code. 'It was so simple when you looked at it that a child could have given you the answer. You count the Os—3114—put the 50 at the end and you have got a Geneva telephone number.' Connell admitted that he had been told to ring this number if the Amsterdam coup succeeded.

The detectives telephoned the Geneva police and gave them the number. It turned out to be the hotel where the carriers were picking up the gold for shipment to Hong Kong. In the hotel the police caught 'L', the syndicate's Geneva agent, together with one of the carriers and the remainder of the money.

The story that 'L' told to the Swiss police was quickly passed on to Toorenaar in Amsterdam. It was that three carriers were already on their way to Hong Kong with gold: 'L' had not been able to buy enough to send the fourth carrier with them.

Toorenaar passed the information over to the Hong Kong police. Two Britons, Anthony Hurd and David Sullivan, were picked up at the President Hotel with gold worth £27,500 at official rates. In Hurd's room the bars were found in his smuggler's vest which he had hung up in the wardrobe. Sullivan's gold was found in an airline bag. The third carrier 'B' (he was never charged) had obeyed the instructions given to him in Geneva by leaving the gold under the mattress in his bedroom and going for a walk.

The police picked up 'B' when he returned, and escorted him down into the lobby of the hotel. Smith, who had an arrangement to meet the carriers, was drinking in the lounge. When he saw this procession he disappeared out of a side door and was not caught until a week later.

From the documents he had found in Connell's possession Toorenaar now knew that the head of the ring in Hong Kong was a Ben Smith. He called the police there and told them to look for Smith at the President Hotel.

The police found his room and kept watch on it for two days but he failed to show up. They went in, and again found a caseful of incriminating documents. One was a telegram, un-signed, from Korea asking: 'Did transaction succeed?' Another was Smith's own bank account which showed a $10,000 deposit from an American in Seoul.

The Bank of America in Seoul checked the account kept in this man's name. There was an entry showing payment of $10,000 to a Mr. Smith in Hong Kong—the money used to float the scheme.

. . .

Toorenaar's office at Amsterdam police headquarters became the control centre of this international police operation to catch the smugglers. Each day he and Jagerman held briefings on the telephone with Hong Kong and San Francisco where the head office of the Bank of America was taking an alarmed interest in the case.

The phone bills were huge: one call to Hong Kong alone cost £100. So the Bank of America authorised the police to charge everything to its account. The whole bill came to over £1,000.

The time zones further complicated the handling of the case. California was eight hours behind Amsterdam: Hong Kong was eight hours in front. The Dutchmen could only talk simultaneously in the middle of the night with both ends of the inquiry. Jagerman would take the call to San Francisco and Toorenaar would talk to Hong Kong. In that way they were able to discuss developments and reach an immediate decision on the next move.

By remote control, Toorenaar fitted the people and the places into the pattern of this huge jigsaw. It was a task well within the capabilities of this six-foot tall, sandy-haired man with the fleshy, expressive face. As he tells the story he swivels to and fro in his chair, chewing a plastic spoon, playing with a ruler and sipping at strong black Dutch coffee.

Toorenaar is the son of a detective from the Hague. He says cynically: 'If you were a Dutchman you could tell where I was from. Amsterdamers say we talk with a potato in our mouths. Anyone who comes from the provinces of Holland is looked upon here as a peasant.' But despite his origins, it took Toorenaar, now forty-four, only fifteen years to become Holland's chief crime-buster.

As one of the souvenirs of the smuggling case he picked up one of the carrier's 'corsets' which he keeps hanging in a wardrobe in his office, next to his ceremonial scarlet, gold-braided police jacket. Unlike most detectives he enjoys wearing uniform. This is probably the result of his three years service as a military policeman in Indonesia just after the Second World War.

The 'golden corset' worn beneath a baggy suit can carry forty-eight half kilo bars of gold, each worth about £500 in the 'free' markets of the Far East. The papier-maché material is fastened round the body by a series of buckles and a zip. For extra strength a harness is draped like a pair of braces across each shoulder. There are three rows of sixteen pockets each with paper inner linings running round the sides. The waist and thigh bear the weight: if the bullion were placed higher up on the chest, the unequal weight distribution would make the carrier top heavy. Although the garment looks as flimsy as a paper bag it could, and did, carry over fifty pounds of bullion at a time.

On the Sunday night, after alerting the Swiss police, Toorenaar and Jagerman again confronted Connell, seeking the name of his accomplices. Connell agreed that he was only one of a group. The leader was a man named Roderic Knowles. 'I met him on Friday afternoon and he told me to go back to the bank on Monday.'

Where was Knowles now? 'He has gone back to Brussels. But he's returning on Monday to take the diamonds and the rest of the cash. I'm meeting him at ten-thirty tomorrow morning on the Rembrandtsplein in a restaurant called 'The Brewer's Shield'.

The detectives asked Connell to come with them the next morning to point out Knowles. 'But he refused, as he had every right to. He said, "I've told you enough already." He didn't want to be the traitor, the Judas, putting the finger on his friend.'

Toorenaar asked Connell what Knowles looked like. The

Australian repeated his story of the 'typical Englishman' — tall, well-dressed, dark suited.

Then Toorenaar went to the restaurant to set up a trap to catch Knowles when he walked in. 'When we got there the restaurant manager said they were closed on Monday morning. So that plan went out of the window.'

Toorenaar wondered whether Connell had laid a false trail to lead the police away from Knowles. He went back to the Australian but Connell stuck to his story of the meeting in 'The Brewer's Shield'.

'After that we weren't very certain what to do. We didn't know where Knowles was staying in Brussels. If they had really arranged to meet in the café and Knowles turned up to find that it was shut we surmised that he would ring Connell to see what had happened.'

Toorenaar went back to Connell's lodgings and asked 'Aunt Martha' to tell the police if she got a call from an Englishman asking for Mr. Robinson. On Monday morning two detectives went to the house, two more waited in a disguised police car on the square while Toorenaar and Jagerman walked up and down among the crowds on the Rembrandtsplein looking for the 'tall, typical Englishman'.

At ten o'clock the police car radio was alerted that an Englishman had just rung Connell's lodgings. 'We were standing there looking up and down and I saw a man coming out of a phone kiosk. It was just possible he was the caller but we didn't want to pick him up on so slender a link.'

Toorenaar went up to the man. He was tall as Connell had described, so tall that he loomed over even the rangy Dutch detective. But he was not a 'City gent' from the cut of his smart lightweight suit. Toorenaar had suspected that Connell was 'leading him on' over the description, trying to cover up for the other man.

Toorenaar asked him in Dutch 'Have you got a light?' But the man made no reply and started to walk off. 'If he had said something I would at least have known if he was English. But we were still no wiser.'

As the man walked away, Toorenaar, posing as a hotel tout, asked in English: 'Do you want a nice hotel, sir?' The man answered nervously: 'No, no. I've already got a hotel.' He was walking away when Toorenaar called after him: 'Hey, Roderic!' Instinctively, Roderic Knowles turned to see who was calling his name.

It was an old trick—but it had worked. Knowles was taken to the police car. 'It was only when we got him inside that we knew why he was so nervous. It wasn't so much the police he was worried about. It was the fear of being picked up by a rival smuggling gang.'

Knowles told the police later that until he heard the police radio he thought he had been abducted by another smuggling ring. It was a common hazard in that business, being picked up by rival gangs and robbed. When Knowles heard the crackle of the police wireless he knew he was finished. Yet he said it was almost a relief to know he was in the hands of the police.

In the police car, Knowles began to cry. 'I felt quite sorry for him because he had worked very hard. All the responsibility had been his: the others were only pawns. He had about £2,000 of his own money on him.'

But by the time the car reached the police headquarters, Knowles had composed himself. For two days he refused to talk. He asked what his rights were. 'I'm not saying anything: not my name, nothing.' He demanded a lawyer but Toorenaar explained under Dutch Law the police could keep a man for four days before a lawyer was called in.

By virtue of his rank Toorenaar is an assistant law attorney. He has the authority to put a man in prison for two days. After that the district attorney is consulted and told the facts. If he agrees with the police view he can order the renewal of custody for another two days. After the expiration of the four day period, a suspect must be brought to the public prosecutor. If there is insufficient evidence he is released: if there is a case against him then the lawyer is brought in.

So, as Toorenaar firmly but politely explained to the young

Englishman: 'The first four days are for us.' They were enough
to break Knowles' resistance.

.   .   .

Toorenaar and Jagerman began the interrogation by
asking Knowles about his movements in Holland. Was he
there alone? 'No, I've come by car from Belgium with two
friends.' Where were his friends? 'I don't know.'

Then the detectives revealed to Knowles what they knew.
'We already had enough proof against him, what with Connell's
story and all the documentary evidence we had found in
Connell's possession. There was no longer any point in beating
about the bush.'

Torrenaar told Knowles that the police knew he was involved in a bank swindle. They told him of Connell's arrest
and to prove it produced a photograph of the Australian. 'We
know everything. Now these two friends of yours: are they
involved in the fraud?'

Knowles said he knew nothing of any bank fraud. He and
his friends were in Amsterdam on holiday. Toorenaar asked
what kind of car he was driving. Knowles said it was a Mercedes
but would tell nothing more.

The police searched the Rembrandtsplein and found a red
Mercedes with British number plates in one of the parking bays.
They placed a watch on it and after about three hours saw a
man come out and put some money in the parking meter. He
was arrested and admitted he was in Knowles' party. He said
his other colleague was still in the restaurant. He too was
picked up and they were all brought back to Toorenaar's office.

These were the carriers who were to have ferried the diamonds to Hong Kong. The smugglers' vests which they had been
wearing were taken away from them. In the eyes of the Dutch
law the carriers had committed no offence. 'All they had done
was to come to Holland and sit in a restaurant drinking coffee —
wearing the corsets. If they wanted to wear them that was
okay by us. We kept them for three days and then sent them

back to England.' When the carriers arrived home they were 'received' by Scotland Yard but no proceedings were taken against them: they had committed no crimes in England either.

Even when Knowles was confronted by the carriers he still refused to talk. So Toorenaar went back to Connell, the less experienced of the two, to take him page by page through the revealing entries in his notebooks—names, addresses and telephone numbers. By Tuesday, Toorenaar knew that the information Connell had given was paying off. The Swiss police had picked up the Geneva gold team; Hong Kong had arrested the gold carriers; Smith, although still on the run then, had been identified and his room searched. That in turn had brought to light the man at the end of this 'golden rainbow'— the American in Seoul who had the bank code secrets.

With so much evidence, Toorenaar and Jagerman felt they could now gamble on breaking Knowles' self-imposed silence by telling him the rest of the story. 'We knew everything but Knowles had no idea how strong our hand was.'

Jagerman, even today, regards Knowles as 'a good English gentleman'. He said to him: 'You are a sportsman, you told me, eh? You win or you lose. This time we have the aces. I will make a deal with you. I'll tell you what I know and if I'm right you'll admit it, eh?'

It was a very one-sided deal from Knowles' point of view— 'heads I win, tails you lose'. But he agreed: 'All right, it's a deal.'

So Jagerman talked. 'I drew out on paper the whole scheme with the names of the members in the various countries. Except for the Far East: I wasn't quite certain of the American's part at this time. So I left that name blank and I said to Knowles: "Now I'll tell you where the code comes from".'

'I'll bet you never know that.'

'I took a risk. I said: "It comes from Korea".'

'Yes.'

'And it comes from. . .'

As he mentioned the name, Jagerman threw up his hands to

imitate Knowles' act of surrender. 'It was all over: finished.
We took a cup of coffee and a Seven Up and he told the whole
story. It was the middle of the night by then but we went
right on to the end.'

Jagerman went next day to Knowles' 'operational headquarters' in his room at the Brussels Hilton. There he found
more damaging documentary evidence: the names of the
whole gold smuggling administration and pictures of every
gold carrier. Later the detectives talked over with Knowles
his many mistakes.

Despite his precise warnings to others about never making
business telephone calls, Knowles had made five calls to Smith
in Hong Kong from the Hilton. Although he had tried to
ensure that each section of the ring operated in ignorance of
what its neighbour was doing, the detectives found that many
of the carriers knew other operatives' names and jobs. And
many of the instructions Knowles had given to observe secrecy
and prevent arrest were to Jagerman 'more fitted to a child's
comic'.

In five days, Toorenaar and Jagerman, with the assistance
of the police in Switzerland and Hong Kong and the help of the
Bank of America security investigators, in California, Amsterdam and Seoul, had scotched a crime that had taken five
months to perfect. What remained were the formalities of
bringing to trial the various personalities picked up in the
police swoops.

First, in Amsterdam, Roderic Knowles and Peter Connell
appeared before the Supreme Court where they admitted
complicity in the attempt to defraud the Bank of America of
$150,000. Each was sentenced to fourteen months' imprison-
ment. They completed their sentences in the autumn of 1969.

These two men served their time in the comparatively
liberal surroundings of a Dutch jail where Knowles grew a
beard and spent his time reading and writing. Two of their
most frequent visitors were the men who brought about their
downfall, the 'terrible twins' Toorenaar and Jagerman.

Knowles and Connell were fortunate to fall upon Dutch

'hospitality'. Ben Smith in Hong Kong found that jails there were still run on Victorian policies of austerity and discipline. When eventually the police found him after his emergency exit from the President Hotel he faced six charges of fraud and received a four year jail sentence. Later, he was to write from jail complaining of the harshness of the sentence for a first offence: 'It was a gruesome fate that has befallen Roderic, myself and some of our lads.'

Hurd and Sullivan, the gold carriers caught in Hong Kong still in possession of the smuggled bullion, were each fined £1,000: 'B', who had got rid of his consignment when he was arrested, was not prosecuted but sent back to Britain. The Chinese syndicate which bought the gold was never traced by the Hong Kong police.

In Switzerland, 'L', the Geneva agent, and the carrier caught with him in the hotel, were held for several months by the police. But it was evident that neither knew anything of the Zürich fraud. They too were eventually set free and returned to England.

'John Brown', the alias of the man who brought off the Zürich bank coup, has never been caught although there is a warrant out for his arrest. Toorenaar believes that he returned to England after handing over the $150,000 to 'L' in Geneva. 'Both the British police and myself think that he is hiding out under another name. Although he was the one man to carry out the crime and get away with it, I gather he is almost penniless today.'

For the Bank of America, the most serious aspect of the case—potentially more damaging than the loss of $150,000— was the knowledge that an outsider had been privy to their secret documents. A commission from the head office of the bank went to Hong Kong and then to Seoul. A long and secret inquiry eventually led to the American who had transferred $10,000 to Ben Smith's account in Hong Kong before the frauds began.

This was the man named by Smith and Knowles as the supplier of the secret bank code and the form of words to be used in the telegram. Both also told the police how they had stayed at this man's house, how they had gone with him to the bank to photostat the documents and how it had been agreed he should take a half share of the haul.

But the American was never prosecuted and eventually returned to live in the United States. Proceedings against him were dropped by the Bank of America for a number of reasons: the problem of launching a prosecution in one country relating to a crime that had taken place in another; the expense of such a prosecution and the attendant publicity that would follow.

Toorenaar also supplied Scotland Yard with the list of eighteen Britons who had been involved in the gold running. Although no offences had been committed in England, the 'recruiting agency' in Courtfield Gardens was visited by the police and the London operatives were seen and given an oblique warning as to their future behaviour.

Knowles' fiancée, Jane Coleman, who arrived in Brussels after he had been arrested, was also questioned by the Dutch police. But Toorenaar satisfied himself that she knew nothing of the bank fraud itself. 'She is a charming girl. At her age smuggling seemed more romantic than criminal.'

When their work was over, Toorenaar and Jagerman were each offered $500 by a grateful Bank of America. 'We couldn't accept it—it wouldn't do for policemen to take rewards.' Instead the bank threw a dinner at the Amsterdam Hilton for the detectives, their wives and the commissioner of police. During the dinner, the bank presented a $1,000 cheque to the police orphans fund: 'But then they can afford it,' says Toorenaar with a broad grin.

'The only one missing from the feast was Knowles. He would have enjoyed it: the Hilton was his style of living.'

RICHARD CHITTY: ENGLAND

The London Police Murders

The London Police Murders

SCOTLAND YARD

INTERNAL MEMORANDUM

TO: SIR JOSEPH SIMPSON, METROPOLITAN COMMISSIONER.

FROM: DETECTIVE SUPERINTENDENT RICHARD CHITTY, DEPART-
MENT CI.

SUBJECT: BRAYBROOK STREET POLICE MURDERS.

'IT IS THE WISH OF ALL OFFICERS OF THE MURDER TEAM THAT
THEY ARE NOT TO BE RECOMMENDED FOR SPECIAL RECOGNITION.

'ALL WERE IMPORTANT LINKS REGARDLESS OF THE DUTY PER-
FORMED AND THEIR EFFORTS ARE WORTHY OF THE HIGHEST
PRAISE.'

'Scotland Yard.' The words convey to the foreigner a little
of the 'mystery' of the British as a race: matter-of-fact, undemon-
strative, tight-lipped. Just occasionally a corner of the cloak is
raised to permit outside scrutiny. It quickly drops back into
place before too much of the 'image' is disturbed.

Such a moment was the Braybrook Street killings when three
policemen were shot down in thirty seconds of pointless
massacre. All under a hot and glaring August sky in a West
London back street.

The memorandum from Superintendent 'Dick' Chitty, a
member of what is loosely called the Yard 'Murder Squad',
to his police chief fairly portrays the attitude of this 'silent
service' to its job: the capture of the killers was reward
enough.

There is an aura about Scotland Yard that in the minds of
outsiders sets it apart from all other police forces. The differences are more implied than specific: today, they are largely

fictional. Given the increasing importance of team effort and the emphasis on good scientific and technological aids, there is nothing that sets the London detective on a level above that of his Paris or New York counterpart.

Yet Scotland Yard's reputation among fellow professionals in other countries—the only true yardstick—still stands second to none. It stems largely from the foreigner's admiration of the system of police administration in Britain. Here, the Establishment—politicians, big business, the 'famous' and powerful—cannot influence the course of a crime investigation: political and financial 'wheeling and dealing' has no part in the police appointments structure, while the policeman himself carries out his crime work free of interference of the judicature and the legislature. (From the policeman's point of view this is undoubtedly the best of situations: some people argue that his power is too great but society does have its system of 'checks'—Parliament, the courts, the Press, organisations which watch out for any excesses.)

Most important of all for the British policeman, he is still regarded by the law-abiding majority of the population as something of an 'uncle' figure, perhaps not a friend but certainly not an enemy. Moral support from the public, intangible though it is, means more to the police than an outsider could imagine.

There have been many times, however, when the pendulum has swung away from the police. In the early late 1950s and early 1960s for example. The case of Detective Sergeant Challenor, the Metropolitan policeman who was accused of fabricating evidence against demonstrators, the Sheffield rhino-whip enquiry which revealed ill-treatment of suspects and the Brighton affair, in which two senior detectives were jailed for obstructing the course of justice, effectively destroyed for some years much public respect for the police.

Today the situation is different. It was a tragic but trite comment by one of Detective Superintendent Chitty's personal team at the Yard, Detective Sergeant Bob Berry, that 'it was at the sacrifice of three policemen that the public image went up

300 per cent. It's a rather macabre way of looking at it, I know, but that is how the public reacted.'

Only the shedding of three men's innocent blood in Braybrook Street restored that equilibrium. It was Chitty's task to see that the relationship did not flounder again. It is possible today to trace back to the success of that triple-murder investigation the present accord between the British 'bobby' and the man-in-the-street.

Chitty, one of the 'quiet' men of Scotland Yard, had an awesome responsibility throughout the four-month-long inquiry. There were pitfalls to be avoided in pursuing the criminals: there were new dangers when they had been arrested.

His first decision, within hours of being placed at the head of the murder team, was whether or not to arm his detectives. The three policemen had been shot down quite callously: Chitty reasoned that their killers would now have nothing to lose by shooting it out with the police.

But the British policeman has a rooted aversion to guns. It has been almost an unwritten rule between policeman and criminal that guns are not to be used. To any foreign police force this is merely a sign of weakness. They argue that possession of guns by the police is a deterrent: the British policeman contends that their possession is an incitement to criminals to arm themselves.

The response by Chitty was immediate: the evening of the murders eighty front-line detectives were issued with guns — the only time in British police history that a full-scale murder hunt has demanded the arming of every active officer.

At one time the Yard armoury ran out of guns and more had to be acquired. The guns which were drawn from the stores had never been used before and were still in their original wrappings. Chitty ordered that special holsters should be made so that the arms could be safely worn under a jacket.

It was the first time in a twenty-eight year long career at the Yard that he had ever had to give such an order. 'Was it difficult? Not on your life. I would have every officer under me

armed where there has been a massacre with firearms and I
have reason to believe the men might still be armed.'

But Chitty gave his men explicit instructions about using
their weapons. 'During the whole of the inquiry, not one firearm
was used by any one of my officers. The firearms went back
intact at the end with the ammunition. They were to be used
only as a means of deterrent and self-preservation, *never* as a
means of effecting an arrest.'

Looking back on the crimes, he says: 'They had to be solved
for the peace of mind of police and public. If three policemen
can be murdered in a side street, it doesn't give much chance
to the ordinary citizen.

'It doesn't take long for the underworld to cotton on to new
ideas. If there had been no "end product" by way of arrests
from these murders I think many more policemen would have
been armed by now. You would have had Chicago-type
shooting matches only this time in London.'

.   .   .

The three man crew of 'Q' car 'Foxtrot Eleven'—Detective
Sergeant Christopher Head, Detective Constable David
Wombwell and Police Constable Geoffrey Fox, the driver—
had been on duty since nine o'clock on the morning of August
12th, 1966. They had been together as a team since July,
operating in 'F' Division which covered the West London
district of Hammersmith. Their job was to act in a 'freelance'
under-cover capacity, roaming the area to anticipate crime as
much as detect it. Foxtrot Eleven was the code name by which
their Triumph 2000 car was known to the wireless room at
police headquarters.

At three o'clock that Friday afternoon they received a
message from their operational chief, Detective Inspector
Kenneth Coote, asking them to come and collect him and some
exhibits from a court in central London where he had been
giving evidence. A few minutes later Foxtrot Eleven, now off
the route which would have taken it to the court building,

stopped an old Standard Vanguard estate car in Braybrook Street, Shepherd's Bush.

There were three men inside the car. The police vehicle pulled in front and flagged it down. From that moment on, Head, Wombwell and Fox had only minutes left to live.

Braybrook Street is part of a large London council house estate. On one side of the road there is a large recreation ground, bordered at one end by a railway line and at the other by the walls of Wormwood Scrubs Prison. The Scrubs jail holds many long-term prisoners and has been the scene of many escapes—while the police murders inquiry was still on, spy George Blake vanished over the wall with the aid of an outside gang.

Because of the jail, policemen are a common sight around Braybrook Street. There was nothing special in Foxtrot Eleven's interception of the Vanguard car to attract the attention of the few people—mainly children—who were about that afternoon.

Wombwell got out of the police car and went back to the Vanguard. His first act was to look for the road fund licence on the windscreen of the car: this was missing. The driver, John Witney, wound down his window as Wombwell came up beside him and asked to see his driving licence and certificate of insurance.

His colleague, Head, walked round to the back of the car, scrutinising the other two occupants and looking to see what they were carrying in the car.

Wombwell wrote down Witney's name and address, then that of his front seat passenger, Harry Maurice Roberts.

At this moment Roberts produced a gun, pointed it across Witney at Wombwell, who was leaning in through the driver's window, and fired. Wombwell died instantly from a shot in the front of the head.

Head, who was speaking to the man in the back seat, John Duddy, tried to run back to the police car to escape the gunmen. But Roberts climbed out of the Vanguard and shot at him twice in the street. Roberts' first shot missed, but the second bullet hit Head in the back and he fell dying in front of the 'Q' car.

All this time, Police Constable Fox had been waiting at the wheel of the police car. He had seen his two colleagues shot down but before he could do anything, Duddy, who had also got out of the Vanguard, ran down the near side of Foxtrot Eleven firing three bullets. Duddy's first shot, which entered through the rear passenger's window, did not kill Fox because the bullet was found undamaged afterwards. The next two shots were fired through the open front passenger window. One killed Fox, the shot entering the left side of the forehead and going out through the right temple. Fox collapsed sideways on to the front seat and his foot slipped on to the accelerator pedal. The car, with an automatic gearbox, moved forward with this sudden application of power. Its front wheels ran over Sergeant Head's body and the vehicle came to a halt with the dead man wedged between the exhaust pipe and the ground.

There was just time for the killers to snatch up Wombwell's note-book from his hand. Then they jumped back into the car and reversed backwards down Braybrook Street—the police car was blocking the way in front—continued backwards for fifty yards down Erconwald Street, reversed into the next side turning, Wulfstan Street, straightened up and sped off towards Hammersmith.

In Braybrook Street a group of young children had been playing on the recreation green when the cars pulled up. Among them was eight-year-old Garry Lloyd who lived just across the road. At first, Garry later told the detectives, he had thought it was a film company on location—Braybrook Street with its 'atmospheric' backdrop of Wormwood Scrubs prison walls is often used for filming. But when the shooting began he realised that this was no theatrical stunt.

Garry and the rest of the children hurried across the road to the comparative shelter of the front garden gates. Garry's mother, who had heard the shooting, came out and shepherded the children into the house. When she returned to the front gate the car had gone and the three dead policemen were scattered in and around the Triumph.

On the corner of Braybrook and Erconwald Streets were two witnesses to the 'backwards progress' of the Vanguard — though they knew nothing then of the shooting that had taken place seconds before just round the bend. Bryan Deacon and his wife Patricia were on their way to visit his parents on the council estate. They saw a blue Vanguard reversing in front of them, its exhaust pipe dragging along the ground, sending off sparks. There were three men inside.

Mr. Deacon's first reaction was that it was a prison break. He shouted to his wife, 'Get the number!' and tried to memorise it himself. Mrs. Deacon scrawled the number of the car on the corner of a piece of butcher's wrapping paper: PGT 726. Her husband got the number in his mind as PGT 728. A lorry driver, asleep in his car in Braybrook Street but awakened by the shots, also got the number PGT 728. The police, when they followed up this immensely important clue, checked out both numbers. The scrap of paper Mrs. Deacon had torn off and pushed into the hands of the first policeman she could see was the right one.

The shooting happened at three-fourteen p.m. It was all over and the Vanguard had disappeared by the time the first call reached the Scotland Yard information room at three-nineteen p.m. At that moment the Yard knew only that three men had been shot: the dead men had been wearing plain clothes and nobody knew for a few minutes that they were policemen.

The first alert went out to Foxtrot Eleven — but there could be no answer from that car. Then Foxtrot One Hundred One which was doing escort duty with another vehicle (strictly speaking it should have been out of radio contact with Information Room while on such work) picked up the message. The crew of that car were the first police personnel on the scene. By then the engine of the Triumph had been switched off and the back wheels which had been revolving against Sergeant Head's body had come to a halt.

The street was cordoned off as police reinforcements poured into the area. From Garry Lloyd the detective got the first eye-witness picture of the crime: two or more men getting out of an 'old' car and shooting three other men. Garry, who had been only a few yards away throughout the drama, said that one 'looked like Bobby Charlton the footballer'.

With the description and the number of two cars, the police had taken a huge step forward at the very start of the inquiry.

.   .   .

Detective Superintendent Chitty had only returned to Scotland Yard that day from Gloucestershire where he had solved a murder inquiry. He was number three on call in the Yard's Central Office and had planned to spend the weekend with his wife at their new home in Kent. At three-forty p.m. that after-noon Chitty got a summons to the office of the Yard's head of C.I.D., Commander Ernest Millen. There he was told the story as far as it was then known, the 'rush' messages still coming in from the information room, and asked to take charge.

Chitty phoned his wife to tell her not to expect him home. Then he began to set up on the telephone the administrative apparatus needed for the job: men and machinery, telephones and offices and asked Commander Millen to make certain officers available to form his immediate team.

This initial, phlegmatic reaction to the terrible news is probably the hallmark of Chitty's method of operating. He goes about his job slowly and cautiously. 'You have to be both an administrator and an investigator when you are dealing with a crime of this complexity. It's important of course to know your priorities: any detective's first job is to catch the criminals. You must never let the paperwork interfere with that object. But if you have things set up right you can delegate responsi-bility.'

This explains Chitty's insistence on certain officers being assigned to the case. 'I have a first-class team and I know I can leave it to them. You're really the figure-head when you're in charge of the inquiry. It's your job to co-ordinate everybody else's efforts.'

It was Chitty, with his knack of bringing order out of chaos, who was sent up to Leatherslade Farm, hide-out of the Great Train Robbers, in 1963 after the discovery of the lair with its 'treasure trove' of clues. The evidence recovered there was to be instrumental in convicting some of the men connected with the £2,500,000 robbery.

Early on in the search of the farm, detectives were over-running the place and there was a danger of destroying this advantage over the robbers by not correctly marshalling all the finds. It was essential for the police that a man with great administrative ability should oversee this tedious but vital job. Chitty and his team were sent up to do the 'backroom' work and deserve much of the praise for the convictions which followed in court.

But for a minor difference of opinion with his father when he was a young boy—Chitty admits that he was a 'typically big-headed youngster'—Scotland Yard might never have had the services of this portly, chubby-faced man.

Chitty was born at Chilworth, near Guildford in Surrey, the son of a market gardener. It had been planned that he should go into his father's business. 'But we had a few words: one thing led to another and I left and joined the police. If there hadn't been that spot of bother I should still be in the market garden business, I suppose.'

Chitty wanted to prove to his father that he could stand on his own two feet. He joined the Metropolitan Police one month before the outbreak of war in 1939. After initial training he started as a probationary constable walking a beat in Putney. After war-time service as a navigator in a R.A.F. bomber squadron he returned to the police as a raw detective constable. His first introduction to murder was in the Neville Heath sex killings in the mid 1940s: 'I only had a minor role, mainly running around for my senior officers.'

As exhibits officer in that and many later murders, part of Chitty's job was to attend the post-mortems. 'You were virtually the pathologist's odd-job man, helping him to measure the various parts of the body, put it together again and take away the organs which might be used as evidence in the case. The first time I did this I nearly passed out: but you have to get used to these sights.'

Chitty had had personal charge of fifteen murder investigations at the time of the Braybrook Street killings. He had worked for many months on the unsolved 'nude prostitute' murders in West London between 1964 and 1966. Six women were killed and their bodies left on waste ground. As superintendent in charge of 'F' division where five of the murders were committed Chitty was involved in the operation of running the murder headquarters from Shepherds Bush police station— later to become the operational base for the men engaged on the police killings.

The nude murders ended abruptly in 1966. One theory is that the killer himself died—very much a parallel with the Jack the Ripper crimes in London's East End in the 1880s.

One of the most unpleasant aspects of the police killings for Chitty was his personal sense of loss. He had known all three policemen through his earlier contact with the Hammersmith police area. He had been intimately concerned in their appointments to the job which ultimately brought them into the gunmen's line of fire.

He knew Fox's reputation for being a keen 'thief catcher' and because of his special knowledge of local villains had used him on the 'Q' cars. Chitty had interviewed Wombwell when he was a constable and had approved his transfer to the detective branch: he knew Head personally throughout his police career from the time he arrived in Hammersmith as a C.I.D. 'aid' (probationary detective). Chitty had personally recommended his appointment as detective sergeant and had trained him in crime investigation and interrogation.

When Chitty reached the scene in Braybrook Street, Wombwell was still lying in the road behind the 'Q' car, his right hand clutching a biro. But his notebook and that of

Head had gone. Head was lying underneath the car wheels and Fox was slumped across the front seat.

Trying to reconstruct what had happened, Chitty asked himself why the 'Q' car had been in the back street, away from the route it would have taken to reach the West End from Acton. The answers then were not immediately forthcoming. Even today the mystery has not been completely solved. But Chitty surmises that Foxtrot Eleven must have spotted the Vanguard in another street and followed it to Braybrook Street.

'Whether Fox or one of the others recognised one of the men in the car we can't be sure. But it's feasible.

'Fox could have known Witney, and his record, because at one time they lived close to each other.

'We know what the killers were doing there. They had marked out a vehicle at Acton for use in a future crime — they had been doing some robberies — and their plan that day was to pinch the car. We believe they were also watching a rent collector going from house to house on the estate. What they were going to do was to pull the car on to the grass and plan how to attack him.'

Fox, the driver of the police car, had not been able to get through any radio message before he was shot. His message pad was found on the seat beside his body but there was nothing on that either to tell the police more about the killers.

Detective Sergeant Berry believes that Fox was either trying to radio for help or was hoping to intercept his colleague Head in the car at the moment the gunmen alighted. 'Fox was in a cleft stick. He was trying to steer the car and at the same time work out in his mind whether he could give cover with the car for Head. By this time Roberts had shot Head and before he had any time for evasive action he was shot anyway.

'He certainly wouldn't have driven off and left his mates there: he couldn't have run off. He sees Roberts going up and "bang, bang" at Head who falls. Fox has got sixteen eyes now: he doesn't know which way to turn. We've all been confronted with the same nasty situation: what do you do first?'

One of the questions Chitty had to ask himself at this early stage was what could have possibly prompted such a massacre. A 'Q' car on a routine interception: Wormwood Scrubs only a few yards away: three men killed. The answer then seemed to lie within the prison. 'We could not overlook the fact that this might have been a prison break-out attempt. It seemed inconceivable at that moment that anything less could have provoked such violence. You have to remember that at that time there were a lot of major villains inside the Scrubs.' Among them were members of a London gang, then awaiting trial, who later received very long prison sentences.

But investigations inside the prison showed that it was just a coincidence that the killings had taken place so close to the Scrubs. Later, the police were to learn that the murderers were little more than petty criminals; that panic was the only motive which had ruled them. But for security's sake one potential escapee was moved to another prison.

Some of the three bullets which had been pumped into the police car had broken the windows on their way out through the other side. They had presumably buried themselves on the recreation ground. With lengths of string, the detectives marked out the angles of flight. This still left a large piece of the ground to be searched.

A team of men were set to work on their hands and knees sifting through the grass. The Army sent in a mine detector team—the first of a flood of outside offers of help. The searchers were hindered by the fact that the green had been used during the war by civil defence volunteers. They dug out a number of bullets left over from the war.

But in the end, after three days spent patiently combing the huge play area, three fragments were found: one matched the bullet from an Enfield ·38 which had killed Fox.

.   .   .

Chitty had instructed one team of detectives to search for the killer's car. It was a London registration number and the way to trace the owner was through the Greater London Council taxation records, always available to the police on request. This inquiry was complicated by Witney's failure, when he had brought the car, to register the name of himself as the new owner. Also the tax on the vehicle was out of date.

But the detectives soon established that PGT 728 could not be the number. At nine o'clock on the Friday night, after eliminating two previous owners of PGT 726 from the investigation, the detectives traced its current ownership to Witney, an unemployed man living in Paddington, London, with his wife.

At that moment Chitty was at the mortuary attending the post-mortem. When he arrived back at Shepherds Bush station (popularly known as the 'Bush') Chitty was told that Witney had been arrested. 'It was about midnight then. I said, "Bring him over". It was one o'clock by the time he arrived at the Bush. He denied it all. He said he had sold the car earlier that day in a public house. And he stuck to that story throughout the night and for the next three or four days.'

A check on Witney's alibi showed that he was either lying or very confused. He said he had been at a public house at Eastcote, near Harrow, at lunchtime, drinking alone and had later gone to a betting shop. But when this was investigated the police discovered he had been in the public house with two other men; and he had not been seen in the betting shop that day.

While Witney stuck to his story about having sold the car, the police twice searched his home but came away with no evidence. He was questioned several times by different detectives but always maintained that he no longer owned PGT 726.

On the Saturday night, when he was bleary-eyed from lack of sleep and still suffering reaction from the shock of the killings, Chitty held his first Press conference in what was normally the station recreation room.

On the first floor of the Bush station, beneath the yellow strip lighting, he faced the journalists across a billiards table, the balls still laid out ready for a game that had never been played. Chitty, who was not then widely known outside Scotland Yard, was nervous and on edge. He reconstructed the bare details of the crime as he then knew it. Then he finished off this first 'public' appearance dramatically, in a voice that was a mixture of Bow Bells and the countryside: 'This is an inquiry that has got to be successful, not only from our point of view but from the public point of view as well.'

One got the feeling that that night Chitty was speaking to the newspapers purely as an aid to his investigation not in any way to satisfy public curiosity for the facts. He refused to say at that stage if a man was being held — yet Witney had already been inside for almost twenty-four hours.

Witney never succeeded in convincing Chitty or his colleagues that he was telling the truth. To break the alibi, the car had to be found. It turned up on the Sunday on the other side of the Thames, in South London. A lorry driver who had been listening to the B.B.C. broadcasts about the missing Vanguard parked his vehicle in a garage under a railway arch in Vauxhall.

On his way out of the narrow cul-de-sac he glanced through the slats of the door to another garage. He saw a Vanguard with a large tyre rolled across the number plate, obscuring it. He called the police and when the tyre was rolled away they could clearly see the registration: PGT 726.

Chitty established that Witney had rented this garage from the owner. In the car the police found overalls belonging to Witney, a pair of car number plates (for use on the vehicle they wanted to steal) and two recently fired ·38 cartridges. There were fingerprints all over the car, including Witney's.

Chitty reasoned that Witney's story about selling the car must now be untrue. If he had sold it what was it doing still in his garage? Why leave his own property inside if the car was no longer his?

'We went back to Witney. We didn't tell him in so many words what we knew. You wait for him to tell you.' But Witney at that stage 'shut up and was saying nothing'.

Chitty arranged for the owner of the garages, who said he had seen the Vanguard driven in on the Saturday night, to try to pick out Witney. But the man said he could not. Then the detectives brought in a thirteen-year-old girl witness from Braybrook Street. Chitty was stunned when she too said she could not recognise the man who was behind the wheel of the estate car. She said the man she remembered 'had more hair'.

This perplexed Chitty at first. Then he remembered that the Friday had been a sunny day and that Braybrook Street ran directly east to west.

'The position of the sun at that time of the day would cast a shadow over the driver. We looked at the Vanguard again. It had one of those full-length sun visors. This explained why the girl thought the driver had more hair: the shadow of the visor would be lying directly on Witney.'

By the Monday, Witney had been in custody for three days. The evidence was mounting slowly but it was still circumstantial. Chitty was well aware of the burden that went with the job. The killings had shocked the public as no other murders had in the last decade. The wave of public support was being translated into real terms which in itself was threatening to be an embarrassment. Everybody was offering help from the Armed Forces to the local girl guides. And money, pennies from children, shillings from their parents and cheques from anonymous donors, was rolling in to every police station in the land.

But the public wanted the culprits so desperately that emotion took the place of reason with street-corner petitions echoing the sentiment: 'Bring back the rope.'

Until the passing of the Murder (Abolition of Capital Punishment) Act in 1965, six categories of murder still qualified for hanging: among them, killing a policeman or a prison officer, or a shooting crime.

In the climate of opinion of August, 1966, with M.P.s pressing for the restoration of hanging and Press and television resurrecting the age-old debates on the merits and demerits of capital punishment, the three killers would certainly have been executed had hanging still been judicially permissible.

Detective Superintendent William Marchant, who as head of 'F' Division held Chitty's former job, was on holiday when the killings occurred. He telephoned Commander Millen at Scotland Yard offering to come back straight away. But the investigation had gone too far by then: it would have been

folly to change leaders in mid-stream. Besides, the British
system of criminal detection—unlike some foreign forces—does
not encourage chopping and changing the investigating team
unless something drastic happens.

The then Home Secretary, Mr. Roy Jenkins, visited the
murder headquarters at Shepherds Bush to meet the detectives.
The Commissioner of Police at that time, the late Sir Joseph
Simpson, called to see Chitty and his men several times. He
discussed with Chitty the legal aspects of holding Witney any
longer without charging him. 'I realised I had either to charge
him now or let him go. It was as simple—and as difficult—as
that.'

Today Chitty is willing to admit that the evidence he had at
at the time was flimsy by court standards. There was the
evidence of the girl and the sun visor: the Bobby Charlton
story—'Witney was a dead ringer for him'—the links with the
car, the cartridge cases and Witney's alibi which had been
proved to be false. 'On top of that, I had to remember that he
refused to say anything. If he refused to talk to me I was giving
him the chance to say it to the magistrate.'

At eight o'clock on the Monday night, the charges of killing
the three policemen were read out to Witney. Shortly after
midnight, Witney asked to be taken from his cell to see Chitty.

'He didn't know what evidence I had, whether I had caught
the other two or not. If you want information from anyone
when you are investigating a serious crime you never tell them
what you know. I certainly didn't tell him I had *not* got the
others inside.'

In this way Chitty had sown the seeds of self-destruction in
Witney's mind. Witney had been charged alone with committing the murders: this meant the others had not been
caught; it also must mean that the police felt they had enough
evidence to proceed against him.

So Witney came up from the cells, anxious to get his story in,
concerned that he should not take the rap for everything that
had happened. 'He wanted to make it clear that he had only
driven the car and had not been so involved in the killings them-

selves as his companions. After that he was like a man getting a great big burden off his mind. He went back and slept like a child for the first time in three days.

'Nobody was in a position at first to disprove Witney's story that he had been a "sucker" — just the driver for the other two. But later on, Duddy's evidence and that of Roberts certainly didn't tally with that.

'From his wife's point of view Witney had been an industrious husband, going out to work every morning in his overalls. It was very difficult for us to shake his story about selling the car. If a man can deceive his wife he is half-way to winning: how much easier it is for him to convince anyone else — even a policeman.'

Witney implicated the others in his statement almost without realising it. 'It's a matter of approach, to know without pushing too much who are the others who are involved. He told us where they lived but not the precise address.'

Witney described what had happened after the shooting. 'After they got the van back into the arches they all went to Duddy's place, discussed what they were going to do and got rid of the police book Witney had taken. Witney said he had to go home and act normally; Roberts intended to go to Bristol where he had friends and Duddy, who by this time was a very frightened man, said he was going to clear off to Scotland.'

After making his statement, Witney was smuggled into an ordinary car which Chitty had arranged to be drawn up at the back door of the Bush station. As a police car ostentiously drew away from the front entrance to act as a decoy for the reporters outside, the vehicle with Witney inside, lying on the floor, was driven out of the back. He directed the detectives first to a block of flats in Maida Vale where Harry Roberts lived with his wife; then to Ladbroke Grove and another flat block, the home of John Duddy.

Chitty's gamble — that charging Witney would frighten him into an admission — had paid off.

.   .   .

Unknown to Witney—and a fact never before revealed by the police—Scotland Yard were on to the ringleader of the gang, Harry Roberts, even before they had found the Vanguard: long before Witney mentioned his name for the first time.

'By the second day of the inquiry we were out at Roberts' place and had picked up his Daimler car which was parked outside. Once we had found that car, its trail led us along the track towards the time of the killing. We were able to build up a picture of the people he was close to; we knew where the Daimler had been seen the day of the killing; where they had transferred from the Daimler to the Vanguard. The association was built up even before Witney opened his mouth.'

This information had come from the 'soundings' 400 London detectives had taken of their criminal contacts and informers. The killings had caused a furore in the London underworld because they meant that almost every criminal in the Metropolis would be quizzed. Almost certainly, somebody had mentioned a name and a car to a detective to prevent the tidal wave of police investigation from disturbing his 'business'.

The police even knew that the bag which contained the guns had been in the Daimler when the three men set out in the morning and that Witney had carried them into the Vanguard.

Six days after the shootings, the second man, John Duddy, was picked up in Glasgow. Duddy's father was an ex-policeman and the family was well known to the police there. First the detectives went to Duddy's home but he had gone to stay with a friend under a false name. The Glasgow detectives were armed when they broke into the top-floor tenement flat where he was lodging. But there was no need for guns: Duddy came without a whisper. 'He was much the weakest man of the three. He was a villain and had done some time [jail sentences] but his bottle went completely [lost his nerve] when he got down to the Bush'.

Duddy made a long statement saying he had shot Fox in the police car under instructions from Roberts. Another piece of circumstantial evidence linking Duddy came to light long after he had been charged. Together with the false number plates found in the Vanguard, the detectives recovered the invoices for their purchase. Duddy was identified as the man who had ordered the plates and Witney as the one who had picked them up.

Chitty could feel well satisfied at having caught two of the killers inside one week of starting the case. Only Harry Roberts —whom the others had described as the planner-in-chief— remained at liberty. But it was another three months before Roberts was found.

All the police cars operating on the inquiry were linked to Shepherds Bush under the call sign 'Shepherd Unit'. Chitty, as the overall head, was 'Shepherd Unit Leader'—'plus a few other names that used to come over the radio every now and then.'

The police knew from the evidence of a girlfriend of Roberts that they had stayed together on the Sunday night—two days after the crime—at the Russell Hotel in central London. On the Monday morning they had gone to a shop near Kings Cross railway station where Roberts had bought camping equipment. Then they caught a Green Line bus towards Epping Forest where he had got off, disappearing into the woods while the girl had returned to London.

Roberts knew the area well. He had camped many times in the woods as a boy and from his Army service in Malaya was an expert in camouflage and jungle warfare—even in the middle of Epping Forest if necessary.

The Commissioner of Police offered a reward of £1,000 for information leading to Roberts' capture—a gesture unprecedented in the history of Scotland Yard. And the police were inundated with offers of assistance from the public.

There were gifts of bullet-proof vests—'a good idea but you had to be built like Tarzan to wear one: we had bullet proof shields available if we wanted them'—Rank Xerox installed a photocopying machine free of charge at the Bush. 'They said the machine would do so many thousand copies but that we were not to worry because we would never reach that number.

By the time we had done twenty times their estimate it more or less cleared the path of the general use of Xerox machines in the police service.'

The owner of a car identical to the Vanguard offered it to the police so that they could reconstruct the crime. Generosity begat generosity. A car hire firm lent the Vanguard owner another car, without charge.

One of the country's largest car hire firms cancelled all its London hirings and made the whole fleet available for police use. Police were turning up in their off-duty time from all over the country. Two coachloads arrived from Hampshire at two o'clock one morning; messages flowed in from every chief constable in the land offering assistance 'no matter how menial the task'.

But Chitty, holding to the maxim: 'You cannot cope if you cannot control' declined, with thanks, any further police help. 'I had got 20,000 men in London available at a moment's notice.'

Clerks and typists, bringing their own typewriters, arrived at the Bush at the end of their shift at Scotland Yard to see if any extra work was wanted. They worked throughout the first weekend, day and night, without pay. One girl, Chitty recalls, was in tears as she typed the post-mortem reports on the three policemen.

The motoring organisations offered twenty-four hour help in the search. The Hammersmith borough planning officer handed over his ordnance survey maps. A man who knew Epping Forest intimately offered to guide police squads there.

The boy scouts, an Air Force teleprinter operator on leave from his unit, a printer who drove up to the station with his hand-press in the back of his van: they all came offering help. The murders had released an ocean of goodwill upon the police.

The operator of a light aircraft company wanted to send up his planes to scour the countryside for Roberts. A car company sent a chauffer-driven Rolls-Royce down to Shepherds Bush to take Chitty about.

'I never did get to use it: I had to make do with an Austin from the Yard fleet.' Local publicans sent in bottles of champagne for the murder squad. Later on hoteliers in England and from abroad wrote offering free holidays to anyone in the murder team.

In all the police accepted nine offers of help from private organisations. Chitty had to be careful that the public's enthusiasm did not swamp the task of finding the murderers. 'You must be able to control every operation. Any scheme that gets out of hand is worthless. Worse, it's an impediment to your work.'

A separate section, manned by four policemen, was devoted solely to handling the public donations which arrived by hand and by the sackful in the post. So much money was coming in that two local banks offered the use of their staff and counting machinery. In the middle of the investigation the mother of one of the murdered policemen turned up at the station asking to see where her son had worked. Detectives bought flowers and cards to decorate his desk.

Sometimes the enthusiasm of the police themselves was uncontrollable. At one stage a report came in that a man resembling Roberts had been seen getting on to a train at Euston Station. Three units of men got on to the train. 'Before they knew what had happened it had pulled out and they were on their way to Reading. The passengers were astonished to see hoardes of hairy policemen rushing through the compartments. You see, we knew Roberts was armed with two guns and those lads weren't going to go in unprepared. They suddenly realised that they were heading off into the West Country with no money while their cars were collecting parking tickets outside Euston.'

There were almost 10,000 reports — nearly three-quarters of them malicious or baseless — from the public saying they had seen Roberts. He was spotted in the most unlikely places: rowing across to the Isle of Wight in an open boat, in St. James' Park, London, in Germany where the police held a man called Roberts for three days before his innocence could be established.

Many tips came in placing Roberts on planes or at airports. Chitty brought operations at Heathrow Airport to a virtual halt after one report. Another time, Roberts was 'positively identified' at London's Cromwell Road air terminal. All air coaches were stopped and searched. After one coach had been cleared it drove off into the Cromwell Road traffic with two policemen in pursuit: one of their colleagues had been locked in the luggage boot.

Thoroughness was the keynote of Chitty's plan to catch Roberts. He could not afford any gaps in the net which had been thrown round the country. Every passport which had been taken out from August 12th onwards was examined by the police. The total ran into many thousands: but the answer was negative.

Roberts was reportedly seen on a flight between London and Birmingham. There were many 'sightings' coming in from Dublin and Chitty personally went over to investigate the persistent rumours. Once again, his energies were wasted.

Several times Roberts was spotted in Soho, London's night club centre. Strip clubs were raided: the detectives found themselves walking into rooms where prostitutes were working. Sergeant Berry recalls: 'It was quite funny seeing the girls. You would walk in to find the client and the Tom [prostitute] together.'

For the public, the 'I Spy Harry Roberts' game was almost the high spot of the summer of 1966. But there was little humour in it for Chitty and his teams. 'I was overwhelmed by the public response. But I never had the time to go into them. The day wasn't long enough. My main object was to investigate the murder.'

A television company dressed up an actor to look like Roberts. Roberts' wife, a strip dancer, was asked by the police about her husband's characteristics; how he walked, the way he smoked his cigarettes, the way he drank his beer, the places he frequented.

At the beginning of September, Chitty went on television to appeal for help in the search for Roberts—warning the public not to act without first calling in the police. He produced three pictures of Roberts, pointing out his thick eyebrows and bulging eyes. Chitty told viewers that the offer of a reward was to ensure that 'If Roberts is discovered, it will be handled quietly, without bloodshed or any kind of battle and without harm coming to Roberts himself or to any member of the public or policemen.'

To keep track of the sighting, the police drew up plans to see if any pattern of his movement could be established. This was Sergeant Berry's headache.

'We hung a huge map up on the wall of the station but by the time we had obliterated it with flags we decided that it wasn't much use. The reports were coming in fast and furious. You name it and he was there. A lot of the stuff was anonymous, some of it villains trying to cause a bit of trouble. But we had to check every one out, no matter how stupid it was.

'It was quite colourful at the Bush at one time with all those flags. We couldn't foresee how many calls we would get or how long Roberts would be at large. After a couple of months with at least 300 genuine sightings we began to realise that our plan wasn't much bloody good anyway and we didn't know just what to do.'

.   .   .

It was the middle of November—three months almost to the day after the shooting—that Roberts made the blunder which led to his capture.

He had been on the run for so long that for the public, at first spellbound by the story of the pursuit, his name had dropped from the memory. At Shepherds Bush police station itself, another crime had happened which for the moment pushed the chase for Roberts into the background.

This was the escape of George Blake, serving a forty-two year prison sentence for spying for the Russians. Blake escaped over the wall, only a few yards from Braybrook Street, on a Saturday night in October, 1966, by means of a rope ladder.

As if the escape was not sensational enough in its own right, a certain piquancy was added to the story by the discovery of a pot of pink chrysanthemums at the foot of the wall where he escaped. Possibly the flowers were a marker for the escape organiser. Blake was never caught—he is now living quite openly in Russia.

From that time on Shepherds Bush became the administrative headquarters for both crimes—Chitty and Detective Superintendent William Marchant, the man who had missed the Braybrook Street case because he was on holiday, working next door to each other.

In November, a factory in the small Hertfordshire town of Sawbridgeworth was broken into in the middle of the night. The night watchman who heard a crash and saw a man run off called the police. A police dog with its handler gave chase along the banks of a small river in the direction of Bishop's Stortford. At one stage, in Thorley Wood, the handler saw the figure of a man but quickly lost him again the dark.

He stopped a passing motorist and asked for police reinforcements to be called in. The dog handler circled the edge of the wood, met up with other policemen and from the glimpse he had had, it was decided that the intruder was probably from a nearby gypsy camp.

'It was an unfortunate mistake. One of the gypsies, John Cunningham, was arrested and charged with the breaking. But later the charges were dropped and he was allowed to go free.' While Cunningham was in custody his father came to see the police. He told them that John had come across an encampment in the woods the previous day where a wireless was playing.

John Cunningham led the police to the hideaway in Thorley Wood. By then it had been abandoned by its occupant. But the police found a shoulder holster (later they discovered that Roberts had bought the leather with which to make the holster from a saddlers' shop opposite the local police station) and thirty-one rounds of ammunition. The camp had been dug in and camouflaged in military fashion. It had been made from branches which had been driven into the ground and lashed together. The covering had been expertly constructed from a tarpaulin with an outer layer of plastic, made by piecing together fertiliser bags. The whole cover had been painted green and brown to merge with the trees. Around the edge of the tent was a ditch of earth and branches. A crooked chimney to draw smoke from a stove poked through the roof.

The occupant — the police still did not know his identity — had furnished his temporary home and fed himself from a series of break-ins in the district. There were chairs stolen from a boat, the stove had come from a railwayman's hut, Tilley lamps and a camp bed had been stolen from a boys' club. The police also found two suits and some underwear and two transistor radios.

Throughout the first day they kept a watch on the tent in case the owner turned up. On the second day, when it seemed unlikely any longer that he would return, the property was taken away for scientific examination.

The trial of John Witney and John Duddy had opened at the Old Bailey when Chitty, who was sitting in court listening to the evidence, was passed a note. It said that the fingerprints found on a bottle of whisky in the tent in Hertfordshire were those of Harry Roberts.

'We went to the Bush to collect the "commando teams" and swept off to Bishop's Stortford, not believing our luck after all the frustration we had had.' The question in Chitty's mind was whether it was already too late. The first sighting in Thorley Wood had been five nights before. Roberts would have had plenty of time to slip away from the district.

Chitty radioed back to Scotland Yard for reinforcements, including the 100-man mobile unit which specialises in search work. As the rest of the tent was dismantled, their fugitive, unknown to the police, was hiding 1,280 yards away in a barn, across an open field, armed with two guns. 'I should think he had Mr. Chitty in his sights there a bit,' says Sergeant Berry.

At dawn on November 16th, the police squads began to beat

their way through Thorley Wood, leaving some men on perimeter guard. Two of the perimeter watchers, Sergeant Peter Smith and Sergeant John Thorne were told by two farm-hands that they had seen a man come out of a Dutch barn in neighbouring Nathan's Wood two days before. Smith climbed through the bales, covered by Thorne's gun. Through the bales he saw a bottle. He pulled a pile of straw down and saw a small Primus stove, a torch, pots and pans—and a Luger pistol. He pulled another bale of straw away, saw a sleeping bag, prodded it 'and up popped Roberts'. In Roberts' pockets was the loaded magazine of the Luger. And by him in a holdall was a loaded ·38. Roberts' first words to the policemen were: 'Please don't shoot. You won't get any trouble from me. I've had enough. I'm glad you have caught me.'

Later, when he had recovered some of his self-confidence, Roberts told the police that until forty-eight hours before his arrest he had been listening to the B.B.C. bulletins describing how the search for him was progressing. Then the transistor's batteries ran down. Roberts said: 'You would never have caught me otherwise. I would have been off long ago.'

Chitty had by then returned to London for the court hearings against the other two men. When he heard the news he retraced his steps along the now familiar road to Bishop's Stortford.

'Roberts didn't confess immediately: of course he wouldn't talk at the beginning. He was like all brave men. When they are together they are full of courage: when they are on their own they are frightened. All these brave men will shoot without fear of retaliation because they know the policemen aren't armed. But get them on their own, man to man, and they've got the guts of kids of five.'

Chitty got Roberts 'to come across' by confronting him with what the police knew. 'He was only too happy to do so after I had told him that he would be charged with three murders. It's only a matter of experience. Nobody can tell you how to do these things. A confession isn't made with a view to assisting the police, it's only made for the sake of self-preservation. He must have realised that it didn't matter a damn to me whether he talked or kept silent. We had so much evidence against him.'

In his statement, Roberts said he had shot Wombwell because he was afraid the policemen would find the guns in the car. 'I got out of the car as the [second] officer ran towards the police car and shot him. Jock [Duddy] got out of the car and went to the police car and shot the driver. We then got into the car and Jack [Witney] drove back to the arches at Vauxhall. We were going to burn it later.'

This altered the picture the police had of the crimes. 'Duddy and Witney had been in custody a long time when we caught Roberts. Obviously they had spoken together or somehow got in touch by proxy. They put the whole of the blame on Roberts —the organisation, the previous crimes, the fact that he had got the guns. When Roberts gave his side of the story it showed how little there was to choose between any of them.'

There were three guns in the bag when the police stopped the car—an Army ·38, the Luger and the Enfield. Roberts said that he and Duddy had gone to Hampstead Heath on the Sunday after the murders to bury one of the guns. Chitty needed all three weapons for the presentation of the evidence: it was the first time he had heard the story about Hampstead Heath but he did not show his ignorance to Roberts.

'You have to use your loaf a bit. When you charge a man with murder you are limited in what you can say to him. It had to be on Roberts' own instigation that he took us out to the Heath.

'We had got two guns back from Roberts and he said: "Well, now you've got all the guns back." 'So I am non-committal: "Well, have we?" and he says "Of course. Duddy showed you where we put the last one."

'You *don't* say: "Where did you put the last one?" You say: "All right, you show us just where you think it was put".'

Early on the morning after his arrest Roberts took the police to Hampstead Heath and indicated with his foot where the gun was buried. The police dug and found Duddy's ·38. 'Roberts thought he was only going out there to corroborate what we already knew. He was more shocked than anybody when he saw it was still there—and an empty cartridge-case packet too. It was just one of those things: you've got to play cunning with cunning.'

Chitty considers that a detective must always 'keep something up his sleeve'. He says: 'In the course of a case you may come across a fact that will be known only to one other person —the criminal. A detective must not tell anybody, not even those working with him. Detectives like anybody else will gossip off-duty, in pubs or in buses, and quite unintentionally the secret may slip out. Then one day you meet the man who shares your secret—and he must be the criminal.'

Chitty believes too that a detective must vary his approach towards a suspect according to the personality of the man and the crime. 'You deal much differently with a nervous, truthful type than with a right hard villain. A villain will sit and be dumb throughout an interview. You still have to go through the routine of asking the questions. If he doesn't speak, you musn't be put off or take it personally.

'Some people will not answer because they are really frightened or because they want a solicitor present. If they want a solicitor I am the first person to phone up for one. It makes my job easier. If a solicitor advises a client to say nothing that is up to him. If he knows his client is lying or trying to tell lies it puts the solicitor in rather a funny position.'

.   .   .

The trials of John Witney and John Duddy had been summarily adjourned with the news of Roberts' arrest. For Chitty and his team of eighty front-line detectives it was the climax to ninety-five days of unremitting effort. They had driven themselves from nine o'clock each morning until well after midnight with only the occasional day's break in between. Chitty had lost a stone in weight: at the most intensive moments of the case—the first four days leading up to the charging of Witney—he and his colleagues did not see their own homes. They snatched sleep in the station when the chance presented itself and went without a change of clothes. Throughout the inquiry, no policeman claimed any overtime pay, neither did they ever take any of the time owing to them.

But once the pressure was off, reaction began to set in for the detectives. 'It all seemed such an anti-climax at the Old Bailey. You have been steamed up trying to find him and then, suddenly, you haven't got anything to worry about. Of course the moment of catching him was a climax. But then you are left in a void. Something inside you says, "He's in," and from then on it's a trial like any other job.'

Chitty, like most policemen, fights shy of revealing his personal feelings — even in a case such as this where the deaths of three men he knew could never be completely erased from his mind. 'You can't afford to get emotional about a crime, no matter who is the victim. You cannot become personally involved. If you do, you can't do your job properly. It's all a job of work.

'Of course when I saw Witney, then Duddy and eventually Roberts I felt emotion. It's exactly the same as if a member of your family gets ill-treated and you come across the person responsible. What's your reaction? Well, mine is bound to be the same. I can't do anything to him but that doesn't mean I wouldn't like to.

'Of course when I saw Roberts I felt like screwing his neck — for what he had done to my colleagues and for the times he had kept me out of bed.'

Chitty admits today that almost his biggest problem, once each man had been caught, was to protect them from the wrath of others — policemen as well as public. 'We had to bring them back to Shepherds Bush station to be charged. The dead men had all worked there, they had personal friends, their families knew each other and their children had played together.

'Policemen are policemen: they are human beings too. My problem was that I had to put a sufficient guard on the prisoners — no personal feelings could come into it — to protect them against anything that could happen.'

When Roberts was brought to the station in November, the crowd outside attempted to break through the security cordon to tip over the police van. Inside the guard was equally vigilant. 'You never knew when somebody would give vent to his feelings.'

Chitty's fear was that any attack from inside Shepherds Bush station on the three prisoners would be misconstrued by the public. 'At that time the police could do virtually no wrong in the eyes of the public. We couldn't have any incident that was going to upset the applecart.'

Scotland Yard had good cause for apprehension. Once before, in 1959, there had been trouble and plenty of unpleasant publicity over the arrest of a police killer. He was Gunther Podola, a German, who shot Detective Sergeant Raymond Purdy in broad daylight in Kensington. He was later arrested in a hotel bedroom and appeared in court with head injuries. 'We had to protect these men against anything that could happen. There would have been some very nice headlines. "The men appeared in the dock, eyes blacked and arms in slings." It would have been sensational stuff.

'And it never happened,' Chitty adds, emphasising every word.

On December 6th, 1966, Witney, Duddy and Roberts finally appeared together at the Old Bailey charged with the murders of the three policemen. After a five-day hearing, it took the jury only half an hour to find them guilty of all the crimes. The judge, Mr. Justice Glyn-Jones, termed it. 'Perhaps the most heinous crime to have been committed in this country for a generation or more.'

He passed sentence of life imprisonment on each man, adding: 'I think it likely that no Home Secretary, regarding the enormity of your crime, will ever think fit to show mercy by releasing you on licence.' The judge recommended that none of the men should be allowed out on licence until they had served thirty years in prison—one of the longest sentences ever imposed by a British court.

Often a full picture of a crime does not emerge until after a trial, when the 'heat' is finally off and a man can speak his mind without fearing the court consequences. Garry Lloyd, the eight-year-old witness in Braybrook Street, had claimed from the start that the car driver, Witney, at some stage got out of the car and took the pocket-book lying by Wombwell's body. 'This was something we could never prove until after the case. Then it was established that he had done this. It contained his name and address and possibly Roberts.' That book was never recovered. They destroyed it.'

For the police it was one of those rare cases where they were able to claim a one hundred per cent success record. After seeing the three killers jailed, Chitty turned to the task of finding the man who had supplied the three guns—the means to the massacre—to Roberts. He learned from Roberts' girlfriend that they had cost ninety pounds and that the deal had been done in a café.

In February, 1967, a Cypriot, Christos Costas, was charged with supplying Roberts the guns—a ·38 Colt Special, a 9 mm. Luger and a ·38 Enfield. Roberts was brought to the court from prison to give evidence but refused to identify Costas as the supplier. He maintained that an interview Chitty had had with him in prison two months before 'was obtained by false pretences'. It was Roberts' one opportunity in public to show his spleen at the detective who had caught him.

Costas was imprisoned for six years. In the view of the court chairman, the deaths of the policemen lay, indirectly, at his door.

Normally at Scotland Yard, when the file is closed on a major case, the officer in charge draws the attention of the Police Commissioner to the work of his detectives. In this case, Chitty's memorandum to Sir Joseph Simpson specifically ruled out any commendations. 'I asked the men and they felt it was unnecessary.

'I had perhaps about thirty minutes' sleep on the Saturday night—the first time I had closed my eyes since arriving at the Bush. It was the same for my men: they all worked terribly hard and all credit to them. They told me afterwards they were not interested in any kind of commendation. I mean, three of their colleagues had died and they would have done the job in any case.

'It was a prime example of team work—one of those cases where by some miracle we made virtually no mistakes at all. That doesn't always happen. I don't suppose there's a Scotland Yard man who hasn't made some error or misjudged his plan of action at some time or other.'

In spite of the detectives' wish, Simpson visited the Bush at the end of the long inquiry, saw each of 120 men individually and thanked them for their work. It was a thoughtful gesture by Simpson, and a diplomatic one.

Some Metropolitan policemen—not Chitty—felt that he had always been too remote and out of touch with his men low down the chain of command. By this act, and by his involvement in the whole case, Simpson, who died in 1968, became more of a 'real' person to his officers.

.   .   .

The case of the three murdered policemen did more for the image of the Biritish police than years of public relations work could have accomplished. It showed the public what the hidden hazards of police work were. It woke them up to the fact that the criminal gunman is not as rare a bird as we would sometimes like to think.

But history has shown that public support for the policeman is notoriously fickle. Chitty, an arch-realist, admits that it is an uneasy alliance. 'Now it's up, some day it will be down again.'

One of the more lasting monuments of people's reaction to the killings was the establishment of a trust for dependents of officers injured or killed on duty. The holiday camp millionaire, Sir Billy Butlin, set the fund off with a £100,000 donation to the Home Office. United Artists, the film company, gave the Variety Club of Great Britain permission to use a newly finished film for charity premières throughout the country.

Chitty agreed to take part in the fund-raising functions connected with the premières: by an ironic coincidence the film was 'Chitty Chitty Bang Bang.' Chitty swears that the name was purely fortuitous: this has not prevented some leg-pulling in the conference rooms of Scotland Yard.

Apart from that fund, nearly £250,000 was collected from the public for the widows and families of the murdered policemen. Mrs. Fox and Mrs. Wombwell and the mother of Sergeant Head, a bachelor, each received £26,500. The other five-eighths of the money was placed in a trust fund for distribution to Fox's and Wombwell's five children.

Another of the 'clearing up' tasks that came Chitty's way was the share-out of the £1,000 reward offered by the police. The largest share, £300, went to John Cunningham, the gypsy boy who discovered Roberts' lair in Thorley Wood. As a 'thank you' gesture to Chitty, the Cunningham family prepared for the detective a present which they presented to him at Bishop's Stortford police station. It was a sample of gypsy food: 'game' pie (Chitty had mentioned how fond he was of pigeon or blackbird pie). But the Cunninghams, unable to find a bird, had killed a hedgehog instead. The pie finished up in the police station stove where, according to the detectives, 'it smoked and stank to high heaven'.

Sifting through the claimants for the reward money, Chitty came across a number of people who had seen Roberts in the Bishop's Stortford area during his months in the woods. Roberts apparently had gone quite openly into local shops to buy food and clothing. With hindsight, several people said they had seen him and wondered if it was Roberts. 'But none told the police. The ones who should have done weren't coming forward.'

The two farmhands who directed the police to the Dutch barn in Nathan's Wood got fifty pounds each for their efforts. The remainder of the reward money—£600—was not distributed. A separate sum of eleven pounds, sent in by members of the public as a tribute to the bravery of the child witnesses in Braybrook Street, was split among two boys.

Even before the three killers had come up for trial, Chitty had been sent on another out-of-town inquiry. He was asked to take charge of a security case at the Portland atomic energy establishment in Dorset. 'That one gave me a right headache. I lost nearly all my hair down there.'

The Braybrook Street killings was Chitty's last murder inquiry. He was promoted to Detective Chief Superintendent and given charge of the Scotland Yard Fraud Squad. Escape from the rawness of physical crime to the silky world of 'white collar' swindlers has at last tied Chitty to a desk. Today he is Deputy Assistant Commissioner in a Yard administrative post. He has put back the stone in weight that he lost at Shepherds Bush and is now more relaxed, more subdued.

Since the killings, Scotland Yard has vacated its legendary buildings on the banks of the River Thames at Westminster and is now a mile away in a 'matchbox design' building overlooking Victoria. Chitty's office is cut off from the outside world by the venetian blinds which are perpetually drawn to help regulate the air-conditioning: Chitty's is a constant battle against the new ventilation system.

On the wall behind him are the framed pictures of predecessors in his job: on a filing cabinet in the corner is a tray of empty sherry glasses—the reminder of some long ago celebratory drink. In the evening, time permitting, there may be a quick visit to the 'tank'—the bar in the basement of the Yard building. Otherwise, it's home to the Kent countryside.

Chitty, now fifty-three, could retire on pension whenever he wished. To younger detectives in his department it has been Chitty's cry for years: 'When I retire, I'll be able to get down to pruning my roses and catch up on some neglected reading.'

But the distinction of being 'at the top' at Scotland Yard is one that comes to few people. And when it does, it's terribly hard to step down.